Jesus
no equal

a passionate encounter with the Son of God

Dedication

To the younger generation whose passion for Jesus will take them all over the globe so that "every people, tongue, tribe and nation" will encounter Him.

The current movement of God that is pointing students to Jesus Christ has not happened by accident. God works as He wills and when He works, He uses people. This book is dedicated to those youth leaders who have relentlessly pursued their dream to see a ministry on every campus in America and every student reached for Christ: Paul Fleischmann, Dave Busby, Rolly Richert, Doug Clark, Doug Tegner, Billy Beacham, Chuck Flowers, Richard Ross, Monty Hipp, Sue McAllister, Rich Malone, Mike DeVito, Kevin Harlan, Allen Weed, Ginny Olson, Chris Renzelman, Benny Proffitt, Chuck Klein, Bo Boshers, Lynn Ziegenfuss and many others who have remained true to the cause.

Jesus
no equal

a passionate encounter with the Son of God

Barry St. Clair

EMPOWERED™ Youth Products
Standard Publishing
Cincinnati, Ohio

Editorial team: Mark Taylor, Dale Reeves, Doug Tegner, Leslie Durden
Cover and inside design by Dina Sorn

Published in association with the literary agency of Alive Communications, 1465 Kelly Johnson Blvd., Suite 320, Colorado Springs, CO 80920.

Library of Congress Cataloging-in-Publication Data:
St. Clair, Barry.
    Jesus, no equal : a passionate encounter with the Son of God / Barry St. Clair.
        p. cm.
    Includes bibliographical references.
    Summary: Chapters provide readings and exercises that encourage the reader to
    get to know Jesus and the events of his life in a new way.
    ISBN 0-7847-1043-0
    1. Jesus Christ—Biography—Devotional literature. 2. Youth—Religious life. [1. Jesus Christ. 2. Prayer
books and devotions.] I. Title.

    BT306.5 .S75 1999
    232—dc21
            99-049338

Standard Publishing, Cincinnati, Ohio.
A Division of Standex International Corporation.

06   05   04   03   02   01

5   4

Contents

Foreword

As I ran around the toddler room with a little car in my hand, I spotted another boy who looked a lot like me. I waddled over to say "Hi!" I don't remember ever shaking his hand, but I do remember his name . . . Bryan Clark. When my mom picked me up, all I could talk about was my new friend. Little did I know that Bryan would become my best friend through high school. Other friends have come along but none of them could fill the friendship that Bryan and I have shared. He has always been my best friend.

We all have stories like this one . . . stories of how we have found a friend who is always there for us, someone we can see and touch. Remember how it was when you found a girl or guy you really liked? You got a smile on your face just thinking about that special someone. Guys, remember how you talked about the girl to all your buddies in the locker room? Girls, remember how you giggled with your friends about how cute he was? Then, the big moment finally arrived. You got to talk to the person and you felt those huge butterflies in your stomach. It seemed as if you were floating and you couldn't come down. That's exactly how it should be in your relationship with Jesus.

I am one of the student leaders of *Revival Generation*—a movement that encourages teenagers to be bold in their faith on campus, praying for revival to come. We are a generation of teens falling in love with Jesus, a generation that considers Jesus their best friend, a generation that is experiencing revival, one heart at a time.

Barry St. Clair, even though he is not a teenager, is a student at heart. I have known Barry for a few years and have seen firsthand his great passion for Jesus. He has made me want to know Jesus more deeply. Barry is a man who knows what it means to love God. He has experienced the ultimate friendship with the Savior. In this book, Barry invites you to take the ultimate road trip to discover a friend who is closer than a brother. I pray that you will find Jesus in a way that many in our generation have. It takes faith to fall in love with someone you cannot physically see or touch, but if you are willing to take the risk, Jesus Christ will become your best friend.

I am convinced of this one thing: There is something very different about my generation. We know what it means to be hurt. We have gone through tragedies such as Columbine and Paducah. The world is asking how we will make it. The only answer I have is Jesus. This book is a tool to help you fall more in love with Him.

Josh Weidmann, student leader
Revival Generation, Littleton, CO

"Who is Jesus Christ? Can He really affect my life today?"

In his book, *Jesus no equal*, Barry St. Clair addresses these questions head-on with experience, sincerity and a dose of humor. This book shows how our relationship with the Son of God affects all areas of our lives. If you are ready to be challenged by the radical life of Jesus, then this book is for you!

Jesus no equal traces Christ's coming: His birth, life, ministry, death and resurrection, then shows the role He desires to play in our lives today. Can we really trust Jesus with our dating life? Can we trust Him with our relationship with our parents? Will He truly guide my life in this century? Can He use me to impact my generation? This book helps us to honor and love Jesus more and then gives us specific and practical ways to do that.

In a world that encourages compromise and mediocrity, we must be equipped to make a difference. *Jesus no equal* gives us the tools we need to stand strong. Barry has created a unique blend of how Jesus not only satisfies the heart, but also the mind. It has truly hit the mark on what it means to be a disciple of Jesus in the twenty-first century!

Josh and Sean McDowell,
Josh McDowell Ministries

Introduction
The Ultimate Road Trip

We loaded up the car and headed south. My son, Jonathan, and I had planned a road trip. It included skipping a couple of days of school at the end of his senior year. (Something about getting out of school made it more exciting!) We traveled light, had some great snacks and drinks, popped in some CDs. We rolled the windows down and let it rip.

For three days we hung out at the beach and the pool, caught the rays, ate at places like "Jack's Shrimp Shack," went for long runs, went out late to get milkshakes and slept in later than usual. We laughed a lot and had some serious talks. But our main purpose for the trip was to spend time together focused on Jesus Christ.

Going someplace together and hanging out is fun. Being together made us better friends. But having Jesus as the focus of our conversation made it the ultimate road trip!

The purpose of this book is to take the "ultimate road trip." You may decide to embark on this journey during your summer vacation. But no matter when you get to know *Jesus no equal,* you will experience the two huge goals of any road trip: fun and friendship. Our desire is to have a fun time every day building a friendship with Jesus Christ.

It won't be the first road trip taken with Jesus. In one account in the gospel of Luke (24:13-35), two men went on that ultimate road trip. Along the way they realized some very important things about Jesus of Nazareth. Toward the end of the trip, *"their eyes were opened"* and they recognized that Jesus had been with them all the time!

On the road they discovered several really neat things about Jesus that radically affected their lives. Those same things we can discover as we study together! They found out that Jesus is:

- a prophet (verse 19)
- a man—Jesus of Nazareth (19)
- a man of powerful words and actions (19)
- a man who was dead (20)
- a man who came back to life (21-24)
- a man who expressed God's glory and changed lives (26, 32)

By the time they got to the end of their trip, *"their eyes were opened, and they recognized him"* (31). That sure is what I would like to see happen to you as you hang out with Jesus—that your eyes would be opened as you discover something new about Him every day, and that you will recognize Him and experience Him for who He really is—the One who had NO EQUAL!

Load up the car and let's get rollin'!

Take the Big Challenge

This book is designed to challenge you deeply! More than anything else it will challenge you to know and follow Jesus Christ. The brilliant C. S. Lewis made the challenge clear:

"A man who was merely a man and said the sort of things Jesus said would not be a great moral teacher. He would either be a lunatic—on the level with the man who says he is a poached egg—or else he would be the Devil of Hell. You must make your choice. Either this man was, and is, the Son of God; or else a madman or something worse."[1]

—C.S. Lewis

Jesus wants you to know Him for who He really is, not who you think He is, who you want Him to be or who your friends think He is. And once you know Him, He wants you to follow Him passionately. But it's not always easy to become friends with someone whose face you can't see and whose voice you can't hear and whose hand you can't touch.

That's the reason for this book—to help you know Jesus more intimately and follow Him more passionately—to have an intense encounter with the Son of God. So how can you use *Jesus no equal* to help you do that? How can you max out this book?

The challenge to you is to spend at least 30 minutes a day discovering Jesus. To do that will take everyday effort on your part. Take the following steps each day in your journey to really get to know Jesus:

- Pray before you begin each session. You can use this prayer: "Jesus, help me to know You better."
- Read one chapter of the book each week for six weeks. Read it at your leisure. If it takes you longer than six weeks, that's okay. Enjoy it.
- Spend 20-30 minutes every day working on the devotional for that day. It's best to do it first thing when you get up, but if you're a night person, God can work with that too.

Read the entire devotional, even if it takes you more than six weeks to get through it. Each study is designed to challenge you. If it is too long for you, then divide it in half or split it into three parts: **Checking It Out** (day 1), **Getting the Point** (day 2) and **Looking Inside** (day 3).

The point is to travel on this ultimate road trip at your own pace. Think about what you read.

- Write down your discoveries. Each devotional is designed for you to respond to what you are discovering about Jesus. Follow these instructions for each devotional. In the **Checking It Out** section, under "Hot Notes," either rewrite the verse(s) in your own words or write them out word for word. The point is for you to get that verse clearly in your mind so you will remember it. Most of the information is in the **Getting the Point** section. Under "Heavy Thoughts," record some brief notes about what you discovered in an easy-to-remember form.
- Express in writing a prayer at the end where it says "Dear Jesus." Tell Jesus what you have on your mind and in your heart about your discoveries. This can be in the form of a question, a feeling, something you are thankful for, an issue you want to pray about—whatever is on your mind.
- Apply what you have learned by writing down one specific way you can be "Jesus with skin on" to the people around you. Be specific and practical. Try to write something you can do that very day.
- Look for places you see Jesus during the week. Either at the end of the day, every few days or at the end of the week, reflect back and jot down all the places you have seen Jesus at work: in creation; in your home and family; in your friends; in circumstances; in answered prayers; at church; and anyplace else He is working.
- Tell your friend(s) about Jesus by going through this book with them. Get another copy of *Jesus no equal* from your youth leader or order it at a bookstore, give it to your friend(s) and then meet with them once a week to talk

about what both of you are discovering about Jesus.

- Attend the youth group or cell group meetings where your leader will have several sessions talking about *Jesus no equal*. Use that as an opportunity to express your thoughts about what you have discovered personally during your encounter with Jesus.

Count Zinzindorf, one of the great followers of Christ in the 1700s made this statement: "I have but one passion; it is He [Jesus], He alone."

My hope for you and your generation is that those will become your words. My dream for you is that Jesus, who has no equal, will become so much a part of your life that you will know Him, honor Him, follow Him and reflect Him in such a way that He uses you to change the world!

One Solitary Life

Here is a man who was born in an obscure village, the child of a peasant woman. He grew up in another obscure village. He worked in a carpenter shop until He was 30. Then for three years He was an itinerant preacher. He never wrote a book. He never held an office. He never owned a home. He never had a family. He never went to college. He never put His foot inside a big city. He never traveled 200 miles from the place where He was born. He never did one of the things that usually accompanied greatness. He had no credentials but Himself. He had nothing to do with this world except the naked power of His divine manhood. While still a young man, the tide of popular opinion turned against Him. His friends ran away. One of them denied Him. He was turned over to His enemies. He went through the mockery of a trial. He was nailed to a cross between two thieves. His executioners gambled for the only piece of property He had on while He was dying—and that was His coat. When He was dead, He was taken down and laid in a borrowed grave through the pity of a friend.

Nineteen wide centuries have come and gone, and today He is the centerpiece of the human race and the leader of the column of progress. I am far within the mark when I say that all of the armies that ever marched, all of the navies that were ever built, and all of the parliaments that ever sat, and all of the kings that have ever reigned, put together have not affected the life of man upon this earth as powerfully as has that "One Solitary Life."

—Author unknown

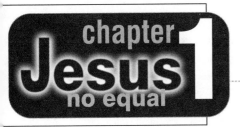

Blind Dates and a Great Introduction

My first blind date: a wipeout! When the guys told me about my date, I got excited. Their description: fine-looking, lots of fun and a great personality (that should have been a hint)!

At 8:00 P.M. we drove over to meet our dates. I tried to be cool, but I was nervous. Sweaty palms and pits were a dead giveaway. As we waited for our dates, this gorgeous girl came out. She's the one, I thought as my heart pumped faster. But she wasn't. Neither was the next beauty who came through the door. Or the next one. Then someone came out who looked like a cross between the dorm housemother and the janitor. That was *my* date!

Disappointed didn't even come close to describing how badly I felt. And I could tell pretty quickly that my date wasn't that impressed with me either.

As I reflected later, I could have had an enjoyable evening if I hadn't built up false expectations. I've found that people have false expectations about Jesus too. Those expectations affect what a person thinks about Him—sometimes forever.

Wrong Impressions

The way I met my blind date is the way many people are introduced to Jesus. They have been told certain things about Him that have given them all sorts of wrong impressions. The difference between my blind date and the wrong impressions people have about Jesus: people usually hear all bad things about Jesus, when the truth is that He is absolutely good. Wrong impressions make it hard for people to appreciate the real Jesus.

Wrong impression #1: "God is out to get you."

Many people think of God as the celestial Scrooge who sits in the sky with His big stick. Every time you get out of line—whack! whack! whack!—He clobbers you. And if you decide to do what He wants, He will send you to "Bunga Bunga Land" to preach on a street corner.

Wrong impression #2: "Following Jesus means you are a wimp."

Some people think of Jesus as this weak, pale Jewish fellow who died 2,000 years ago. The assumption: "Following Jesus means I must wear a dorky-looking suit and tie, carry a 50-pound King James Bible and hang a sign on my back that says, 'Beat me up; I'm a Christian wimp.'"

Wrong impression #3: "Following Jesus means keeping tons of rules."

Ask the average person on the street what it means to be a Christian and he will probably answer, "Christianity is a bunch of rules." Too many people think that following Jesus means to *stop* doing the ten things they like most and to *start* doing the ten things they hate the most.

Wrong impression #4: "Following Jesus is an emotional high."

If a person cries, gets "a warm feeling in his heart," jumps up and down at a concert or experiences an awesome week at church camp, then that person is a follower of Christ. Not really. A follower of Christ can have strong emotions, but following Jesus is much more than emotions.

Wrong impression #5: "Following Jesus means going to church."

Contrary to popular opinion, God does not live in a box with a steeple where people go to visit Him every Sunday. As important as the church is, God is not limited to a church building. He is present where you live, eat, sleep and work. Going to church doesn't make you a Christian any more than going to McDonald's makes you a Big Mac™!

Like my blind date, wrong impressions or misconceptions about Jesus can lead to disaster. We need to know Jesus for who He really is—and not miss knowing Him because of a wrong impression.

When you first heard about Jesus, what were your impressions of Him?

A Great Introduction

I walked into the school library and looked around for a place to sit. When I looked over to my right, there she was—the finest looking lady I had ever seen. I wanted to meet her. I took a "check out" position behind a bookshelf, pushed some books around and stared at her.

Big problem: she was with a guy. Taking the situation in hand, I walked right up and started talking to the guy she was with. He was a nice guy and had no choice but to introduce me. What a great introduction it was!

After a few minutes, Carol and I started talking. And I kept on talking to her . . . and talking . . . and talking. For all I know, the guy who introduced us is still in the library!

The next night I asked Carol out for a "study" date. Study date defined: carry your books, study for five minutes, then go out and have fun. That's what we did. The more we talked, the more we enjoyed each other. Over the months the relationship developed from friendship to engagement . . . then to marriage and four wonderful kids.

This was totally different from the blind date. The difference? We started right with a great introduction.

Starting Right

To start right with Jesus, we need a great intro, a solid relationship, fun and enjoyable times together, deepening the friendship. In the process we get a much better understanding of who Jesus really is.

The reason we can have that kind of relationship with Jesus is because of the way He introduced Himself to us. How did He do that?

• He came from His Father.

"In the beginning was the Word [Jesus], and the Word was with God, and the Word was God. He was with God in the beginning" (John 1:1, 2).

• He came to live with us.

"So the word of God became a human being and lived among us" (John 1:14, Phillips).

• He lived like all other human beings.

"And as Jesus continued to grow in body and mind, he grew also in the love of God and of those who knew him" (Luke 2:52, Phillips).

Jesus went through His teen years just like all of us. I wonder what teenage problems He suffered through. Legs that looked too long? Feet too big? Squeaky voice? Pimples? He grew up facing all of the same issues we face. When He got hungry, He wanted to eat. When He got thirsty, He wanted something to drink. If His sandals rubbed His toes, He got blisters. He even struggled with pleasing His parents (Luke 2:41-51).

- ## He was a man's man.

  "Isn't this the carpenter?" (Mark 6:3).

  Jesus worked hard. He had callused hands and hard muscles from His work as a carpenter. He didn't worry about getting a little dirt under His fingernails.

- ## He came to identify with us personally.

  "Now Christ is the visible expression of the invisible God" (Colossians 1:15, Phillips).

  Jesus gave us an exact picture of God. He came so we could see who God is. When we look at Jesus Christ, that is exactly who we see—God! And when He looks at us, He can see the potential of *"God in us."*

  He came and introduced Himself because He wants us to know Him!

Check Your Introduction

From what you just discovered, check the boxes that best describe how you view Jesus.

- ☐ Jesus was an afterthought God had.
- ☐ Jesus was a Band-Aid® God slapped on a messed-up world.
- ☐ Jesus was around from the beginning and a part of God's original plan.
- ☐ Jesus was a quick fix to counter the power of Satan.
- ☐ Jesus was a great reminder of what God is like.
- ☐ Jesus is all God and all man.
- ☐ Jesus is half-God and half-man.
- ☐ Jesus is so far above us that we can't relate to Him.
- ☐ Jesus wasn't anything like the kids of His day.
- ☐ Jesus could not possibly have had zits.
- ☐ Jesus was so perfect as a child that no one could relate to Him.
- ☐ Jesus was admired and respected by all.
- ☐ Jesus had all the same human desires we do.
- ☐ Jesus had some of the same human desires we do.
- ☐ Jesus had none of the same human desires we do.
- ☐ Jesus was God, so human desires were not even an issue.
- ☐ Jesus reminds us of God.
- ☐ Jesus was so much like God that we can look at Him and see God.
- ☐ Jesus and God were entirely separate from each other.
- ☐ Jesus existed after God did.

Powerful Claims

On the busiest intersection in a city stands a man wearing a blue uniform, a beaked cap and a whistle around his neck. When that police officer directs a tractor trailer to turn right, it turns right. However, if a senior at your school goes out there wearing a T-shirt and jeans, and blows a whistle, he'll probably have a little sports car leave tire tread marks on his face. The police officer may have no more physical strength and power than the student, but he has authority—the delegated power of the police department, of his state and of the United States government.

Jesus had God's authority. That's why He could make the claims He did and then back them up. Right now, forget all "the stuff" you have heard about Jesus in the past. Check out some of His claims and see what He says about Himself.

• Jesus claimed to have the power to forgive sins.

Teaching in a friend's house one day, a crippled man was lowered into a crowded room through a hole his friends had made in the roof. Jesus told him, *"Your sins are forgiven"* (Mark 2:5).

Some of the religious leaders said He couldn't do that. Jesus' response: *"Which is easier: to say to the paralytic, 'Your sins are forgiven,' or to say, 'Get up, take your mat and walk'? But that you may know that the Son of Man has authority on earth to forgive sins . . . . He said to the paralytic, '. . . get up, take your mat and go home.'"* And he did (Mark 2:9-11).

• Jesus claimed that God is His Father.

When the Jewish leaders criticized Jesus for healing on the Sabbath, He said, *"He who does not honor the Son does not honor the Father, who sent him"* (John 5:23).

• Jesus claimed to be the only way to know God.

Jesus' disciples were in a state of confusion when Thomas asked Him, *"Lord, we don't know where you are going, so how can we know the way?"*

Jesus answered, *"I am the way and the truth and the life. No one comes to the Father except through me. If you really knew me, you would know my Father as well."* (John 14:5-7).

• Jesus claimed to be eternal.

To a group of skeptical religious leaders Jesus made this claim:

"Your father Abraham rejoiced at the thought of seeing my day; he saw it and was glad" (John 8:56).

When the religious leaders protested that it was impossible for Jesus to have known someone who died hundreds of years earlier, Jesus replied, *"Before Abraham was born, I am!"* (John 8:58).

• Jesus claimed to be God in human form.

The religious leaders asked Him to tell them if He was the Christ. His concluding statement to them was, *"I and the Father are one"* (John 10:30).

Later, when one of His disciples asked, *"Lord, show us the Father,"* Jesus told him clearly: *"Anyone who has seen me has seen the Father"* (John 14:8, 9).

Don't let anybody fool you. They will tell you that Jesus was a great moral teacher, a religious leader or a holy man, but there are many other ways to get to God. False! If these claims are true, then He is a whole lot more. In fact, He is in a class by Himself. How do we know if these claims are true?

Proof Positive

Throughout history people have made claims that they were God, or had a "special relationship" with God—Muhammad, Buddha, Confucius, David Koresh and hundreds of other leaders of cults. The difference between Jesus and all other religious leaders is this: He fully backed up every claim He made!

It's one thing to claim to be God. It's another thing to actually prove it. Let's look at a few of these convincing proofs:

• Jesus said, *"I am the bread of life"* (John 6:35).

He said that after He miraculously produced bread to feed over 5,000 people (John 6:5-13).

• Jesus said, *"I am the light of the world"* (John 8:12).

Shortly after this statement Jesus healed a blind man. He wasn't just a little nearsighted or needed his contact lenses adjusted. He had been blind from birth. Jesus healed at least nine blind people in the New Testament.

- **Jesus said, *"I am the resurrection and the life"* (John 11:25).**

  Jesus made this statement near the grave of His friend Lazarus who had been dead for four days and whose body had already begun to smell. At Jesus' command, Lazarus got up and walked out of the grave alive!

- **Jesus said He would rise from the dead after three days (Matthew 16:21).**

  According to Matthew 28, that's exactly what He did. Three days after He had been nailed to the cross, Jesus burst out of the grave!

Your Introduction

Have you had some wrong impressions of Jesus? If you have, we can make those right in the rest of the book.

Or maybe you have had a great introduction to Him. If so, you will get to know Him better as you go through this study. If Jesus is who He says He is—God's Son who died on a cross to forgive your sins and rose from the dead to give you life—then pay any price, do whatever it takes to know Him!

Up Close and Personal

1. *How did what you read in this chapter change your view of Jesus?*

2. *Have you experienced the great introduction to Jesus? If not, tell Him you want to get to know Him. Say this to Him: "Jesus, I want to know You. I know You are who You claim to be. Through Your death on the cross, please forgive my sins. Through rising from the dead, please give me Your life. I open my heart to You now."*

3. *If you already know Jesus, tell Him you want to get to know Him better.*
   "Jesus, I know You are who You say You are. Thank You for my relationship with You. Please give me a stronger, deeper, richer, more exciting relationship with You every day."

day 1

The One and Only

"After six years given to the impartial investigation of Christianity . . . I have come to the deliberate conclusion that Jesus Christ was the Messiah of the Jews, the Saviour of the world and my personal Saviour."[1]
—*Lew Wallace, 19th century lawyer and U.S. general*

Checking It Out

Place a hundred quadrillion silver dollars two feet deep across Texas, and place a mark on one of them, then stir them up. Blindfold one man and ask him to pick up one silver dollar from anywhere in Texas, but he must pick up the marked silver dollar. The probability of his retrieving the exact one is the same likelihood that the prophets had of writing eight prophecies and having them all come true in one man from the day they wrote it until today. But they all came true in Jesus Christ.[2]

That probability was only for eight prophecies, but Jesus fulfilled at least 109 prophecies!

At the end of His earthly life Jesus said, "This is what I told you while I was still with you: Everything must be fulfilled that is written about me in the Law of Moses, the Prophets and the Psalms" (Luke 24:44).

Hot Notes:

Getting the Point

Read Luke 24:44 again.

Was Jesus unique? The Old Testament prophecies convince us that He was. The Old Testament, Jesus Himself and the New Testament writers all appeal to prophecy to show the uniqueness of Jesus the Messiah.

Prophecy separates Jesus from every other human being who has ever lived and identifies Him with the Messiah.

Heavy Thoughts:

Looking Inside

Do you ever feel unloved because of divorced parents, rejection by a friend, being dumped by the person you date or just having a bad day? The "one and only" loves you!

"This is how God showed his love among us: He sent his one and only Son into the world that we might live through him" (1 John 4:9).

Dear Jesus:

Jesus with skin on:

Totally Unique–Part 1

"Christ is the great central figure in the world's history. . . . All the lines of history converge upon him."[3]
—*Charles Spurgeon, English theologian*

Checking It Out

My driver's license number is 234560018. What's yours? No one else in the world has that number but me. That number separates me from the five billion other people on Planet Earth.

Fulfilled prophecy separates Jesus from every other person who has ever lived. The prophet Isaiah told us that God would give us a sign that would show how unique the Messiah would be:

"Therefore the Lord himself will give you a sign: The virgin will be with child and will give birth to a son, and will call him Immanuel" (Isaiah 7:14).

Hot Notes:

Getting the Point

Read over the information in this section to check out Jesus "driver's license number." You can take your Bible and look up each one of these if you want.

Heavy Thoughts:

1. He was born of the seed of a woman.
- *A virgin gave birth to a son (Isaiah 7:14).*
- *God sent His son, born of a woman (Galatians 4:4).*

Jesus was the only one born of the seed of a woman. Everyone else has been born of the seed of a man and a woman.

2. He was born of Noah.
- *Noah's sons who survived the ark were Shem, Ham and Japheth. They would be blessed (Genesis 9:18, 26).*
- *Jesus was a descendant of Shem (Luke 3:36).*

Since the Messiah would come from Shem's descendants, two-thirds of the world's population is eliminated here.

3. He was born of Abraham.
- *God promised Abraham that He would bless him and make him a great nation (Genesis 12:2, 3). Abraham had Isaac.*
- *Abraham's seed was "one seed," not many seeds, meaning one person—and that when he was 100, one son from whom came the Messiah (Galatians 3:16).*

The Messiah can come from only one race, the Jews.

4. He was born of Isaac.
- *Through Isaac, not Ishmael, Abraham's descendants will be named (Genesis 21:12).*
- *Jesus was a descendant of Isaac (Luke 3:34).*

Abraham had two sons, Ishmael and Isaac. All of Ishmael's descendants are eliminated here.

5. He was born of Jacob.
- *God showed Jacob that he would produce a nation and kings (Genesis 35:9-12). A ruler will come from Jacob (Numbers 24:17).*
- *God told Mary that her son would rule over the house of Jacob forever. His kingdom would never end (Luke 1:33).*

Isaac had two sons, Jacob and Esau. Here one-half of the descendants of Isaac are eliminated.
Tomorrow we will look at the rest of Jesus' totally unique "driver's license number."

Looking Inside

Jesus was born uniquely as the "one and only" from His Father—totally different from any other birth. Although not Jesus, each of us is unique too—no one else in the whole world has the same exact fingerprints as you! You are not "a hunk of junk" or "a piece of trash"—you are special in God's eyes.

"For we are God's workmanship [work of art], created in Christ Jesus to do good works, which God prepared in advance for us to do" (Ephesians 2:10).

Dear Jesus:

Jesus with skin on:

Totally Unique–Part 2

"The greatest and most momentous fact which the history of the world records is the fact of [Jesus'] birth."[4]
—Charles Spurgeon, English theologian

Checking It Out

Yesterday we said our driver's license number makes us totally unique from everyone else. That number separates us from the five billion other people on Earth. Fulfilled prophecy separates Jesus from every other person who has ever lived. The Bible tells us that a child would be born uniquely, and His uniqueness would single Him out as the Messiah.

"For to us a child is born, to us a son is given. . . . He will reign on David's throne and over his kingdom, establishing and upholding it with justice and righteousness from that time on and forever." (Isaiah 9:6, 7).

Hot Notes:

Getting the Point

To continue to see how totally unique Jesus really was, finish checking out Jesus' "driver's license number" from yesterday.

6. He was born of the tribe of Judah.
- *Judah will produce the one who will rule over Israel (Genesis 49:10; Micah 5:2).*
- *It is clear that Jesus descended from Judah (Hebrews 7:14).*

Jacob had 12 sons, each a tribe of the Jewish nation. With this prophecy 11/12ths of the line of Jacob are eliminated.

7. He was born of the family of Jesse.
- *From Jesse will come a Branch, the Root of Jesse, and all the nations will follow Him (Isaiah 11:1, 10).*
- *Jesus was a descendant of Jesse (Luke 3:32).*

Of all the lines of the tribe of Judah, Jesse's was God's choice. All of the others are eliminated.

8. He was born of the house of David.
- *From David will come a righteous Branch, a King, who will save Israel (Jeremiah 23:5, 6).*
- *Jesus is referred to as the "son of David" 12 times (Luke 3:31).*

Jesse had eight sons. The other seven are all eliminated.

9. He was born of a virgin.
- *From the descendants of David, the Messiah would be born of a virgin (Isaiah 7:14).*
- *The birth of Jesus came about when Mary married Joseph, but before they had a sexual relationship. Mary was made pregnant by the Holy Spirit (Matthew 1:18).*

Only one person in all of history has ever qualified to be the Messiah: Jesus of Nazareth. Jesus was totally unique!

Heavy Thoughts:

Looking Inside

Jesus' uniqueness makes us unique because we belong to Him! When we feel disappointed because we never measure up to what other people expect, we can remember that we belong to Jesus, the most totally unique person who ever lived!

"For consider what he has done—before the foundation of the world he chose us to become, in Christ, his holy and blameless children living within his constant care" (Ephesians 1:4, Phillips).

Dear Jesus:

Jesus with skin on:

Personality Plus

"More than 1900 years later an historian like myself, who doesn't even call himself a Christian, finds the picture centering irresistibly around the life and character of this most significant man. . . . Jesus stands first."[5]
—H. G. Wells, historian

Checking It Out

The movie *La Dolce Vita* opens with a shot of a helicopter carrying a giant statue of Jesus to Rome. Arms outstretched, Jesus hangs in a sling. As the helicopter passes over, people begin to recognize him. "Hey, it's Jesus," shouts an old farmer, hopping off his tractor and racing across the field. Nearer Rome, bikini-clad girls sunbathing around a pool wave with a friendly greeting and the helicopter pilot swoops in for a closer look, taking Jesus with him. Silent, expressionless, exuding no personality, Jesus hovers over the scene.[6]

What an inaccurate picture of Jesus! Even the prophecies from the Old Testament show us what a dynamic personality He was.

"A shoot will come up form the stump of Jesse; from his roots a Branch will bear fruit. The Spirit of the LORD will rest on him—the Spirit of wisdom and of understanding, the Spirit of counsel and of power, the Spirit of knowledge and of the fear of the LORD" (Isaiah 11:1, 2).

Hot Notes:

Getting the Point

Talk about personality! Jesus had it. Isaiah tells us that the Messiah actually would have seven significant aspects to His personality:

1. He will be **full of God's Spirit.** The Spirit will communicate all of who God is through the personality of the Messiah.
2. He will be **wise.** Through the Spirit, the Messiah will have God's intelligence and perspective on everything.
3. He will be **understanding.** The Spirit will give the Messiah a practical understanding of how to do things (like be a carpenter, for example) and how to perceive people.
4. He will be a **counselor.** Through the Spirit, the Messiah will be able to read any situation and reach the right decision on what to do.
5. He will have **power.** The Holy Spirit will give Him the ability and energy to carry out these decisions.
6. He will have **knowledge.** This is intimate knowledge. The Messiah will have a total knowledge of who God is and what He wants Him to do.

7. He will have **the fear of the Lord.** The Messiah will have a reverence for God that holds Him in awe. In these seven aspects the Holy Spirit descended on the Messiah and gave Him the personality of God Himself. Isn't that awesome?![7]

Jesus was that Messiah!

"The Word [Jesus] became flesh and made his dwelling among us. We have seen his glory, the glory of the One and Only, who came from the Father, full of grace and truth" (John 1:14).

Heavy Thoughts:

Looking Inside

The Messiah had the most dynamic personality ever. But you may not feel like yours is much. No talent (the only instrument you play is the radio), no brains ("I have an IQ just above plant life"), no fun, no friends. All of us feel this way at times. The great news is that the same Spirit that lived in the Messiah lives in you, if you are a believer in Jesus.

Jesus said, **"And I will ask the Father, and he will give you another Counselor to be with you forever—the Spirit of truth"** (John 14:16, 17).

Dear Jesus:

Jesus with skin on:

Just Do It

"If Jesus had never lived, we would not have been able to invent him."[8]
—Walter Wink

Checking It Out

When I tie the strings on my Nike shoes before I go out to run, I mutter almost subconsciously under my breath: "Just do it." Nike has influenced my thoughts, my words and my pocketbook with that phrase that is recognized everywhere around the world. I'll bet you own something with Nike on it. And I'll bet you have used the phrase "just do it" recently.

Jesus had far greater influence than that when He lived on Earth. People were "amazed" at what He did. Jesus certainly would have worn Nike because every day He went out to "just do it." What was "it"? What did He do? See if you can find out from this prophecy about the Messiah in the Old Testament:

"The Spirit of the Sovereign Lord is on me, because the Lord has anointed me to preach good news to the poor. He has sent me to bind up the brokenhearted, to proclaim freedom for the captives and release from darkness for the prisoners, to proclaim the years of the Lord's favor" (Isaiah 61:1, 2).

The "it" that the Messiah does is ministry to people. *What three primary ministries did Jesus do?*

Hot Notes:

Getting the Point

For sure, Jesus was the Messiah. What was prophesied that the Messiah would do, Jesus did. Isaiah 61:1, 2 says the Messiah will do three things:

1. **Preach good news to the poor.**
2. **Bind up (heal) the brokenhearted.**
3. **Release the captives and prisoners.**

Jesus walked into the Jewish synagogue in Nazareth, where He grew up and gave His first sermon. It was short. He unrolled the scroll and read: *"The Spirit of the Lord is on me, because he has anointed me to preach good news to the poor. He has sent me to proclaim freedom for the prisoners and recovery of sight for the blind, to release the oppressed, to proclaim the year of the Lord's favor"* (Luke 4:18, 19).

Then He rolled up the scroll and sat down. Every person had his eyes glued on Him. Then Jesus gave His sermon—short and sweet:

"Today this scripture is fulfilled in your hearing" (Luke 4:21).

Take your Bible and pick any ten pages in the four Gospels (Matthew, Mark, Luke or John). On those pages, how many times do you find Jesus doing those three things? _____

Isaiah said the Messiah would "just do it." Jesus *did* "just do it"!

Heavy Thoughts:

_____

_____

_____

_____

Looking Inside

So what about you? Can you "just do it" too? Maybe you feel that the Christian life is dull and boring. Nothing could be further from the truth. Following Jesus is not about sitting in church twiddling your fingers; rather it's about taking Jesus to the streets. Is it possible that you can do the same things He did?

His disciples got to "just do it." Notice the three things they did: *"They went out and preached that people should repent. They drove out many demons and anointed many sick people with oil and healed them"* (Mark 6:12, 13).

Jesus, the Messiah, made an incredible promise to you. Because the Spirit of Jesus lives in you, you too can "just do it."

"I tell you the truth, anyone who has faith in me [does that include you?] *will do what I have been doing.* [What has He been doing? 1._____ 2._____ 3._____] *He will do even greater things than these, because I am going to the Father"* (John 14:12).

That promise is for you, straight from the Messiah Himself. Just do it!

Dear Jesus:

_____

_____

_____

Jesus with skin on:

That's Incredible!

"The might of the world, the most sophisticated religious system of its time allied with the most powerful political empire, arrays itself against a solitary figure, the only perfect man who ever lived."[9]
—Philip Yancey

Checking It Out

When President John F. Kennedy was shot and killed on November 22, 1963, the entire world watched it on television. Even though the entire nation watched, to this day no firm conclusion has been reached on exactly what happened, who killed him or why. The evidence doesn't agree. By comparison, that makes the death of Jesus absolutely incredible. What makes it incredible is its credibility! The prophecies concerning the cross are overwhelming in their number and their accuracy. Check this out:

An electron is the smallest known object. If you had to count one inch of electrons, counting 250 each minute day and night, you could count them in 19 million years! To count a cubic inch of electrons, it would take you 19 x 19 x 19 million years. If you marked one of those electrons, stirred them up and then had a blindfolded person pick one, that is about the probability it would take for the 25 prophecies about the cross to be fulfilled in one person.

The Old Testament predicts exactly what will take place 700 years before it happens! (Remember that the founding of the United States happened only 200 plus years ago.)

"But he was pierced for our transgressions, he was crushed for our iniquities; the punishment that brought us peace was upon him, and by his wounds we are healed" (Isaiah 53:5).

Hot Notes:

Getting the Point

Isaiah 53:5 is only one of 25 specific prophecies about the death of Jesus on the cross. Check out these facts. Look up some or all of the verses to see how detailed God was in foretelling the death of His Son.

Prophecies about the Cross
1. Betrayed by a friend (Psalm 41:9; Matthew 26:49, 50)
2. Forsaken by His disciples (Zechariah 13:7; Matthew 26:31, 56)
3. Accused by false witnesses (Psalm 35:11; Matthew 26:59-61)
4. Quiet before His accusers (Isaiah 53:7; Matthew 27:12-14)
5. Wounded and bruised (Isaiah 53:5; Matthew 27:26)
6. Beaten and spit on (Isaiah 50:6; Matthew 26:67)
7. Mocked (Psalm 22:7, 8; Matthew 27:39, 44)
8. Fell under the cross (Psalm 109:22-25; Luke 23:26)
9. Hands and feet pierced (Psalm 22:14-16; Luke 23:33)

10. Crucified with thieves (Isaiah 53:12; Matthew 27:38)
11. Prayed for persecutors (Isaiah 53:12; Luke 23:34)
12. Rejected by His own people (Psalm 118:22, 23; Matthew 21:42)
13. Hated without a cause (Psalm 69:4; John 15:25)
14. His friends stood far off (Psalm 38:11; Matthew 27:55, 56)
15. People shook their heads (Psalm 109:25; Matthew 27:39, 40)
16. Stared upon (Psalm 22:17; Luke 23:35)
17. Garments divided and lots cast (Psalm 22:18; John 19:23, 24)
18. He would be thirsty (Psalm 69:21; John 19:28, 29)
19. Cried out when forsaken (Psalm 22:1; Matthew 27:46)
20. Committed Himself to God (Psalm 31:5; Luke 23:46)
21. Bones not broken (Psalm 34:20; John 19:33, 36)
22. His heart would be broken (burst) (Psalm 22:14; John 19:34)
23. His side would be pierced (Zechariah 12:10; John 19:34)
24. Darkness over the whole land (Amos 8:9; Matthew 27:45)
25. Buried in a rich man's tomb (Isaiah 53:9; Matthew 27:57-60)

Could Jesus have deliberately read the Old Testament and then forced all these things to come true? It would have been tough from the cross to tell the soldiers, "Stick the sword in my side. It's one of the prophecies, you know." No. Almost all of the fulfilled prophecies were beyond His control.

Heavy Thoughts:

_____

_____

_____

_____

Looking Inside

To express His love to us, God designed the cross with painstaking detail. From the beginning of time, God the Father and God the Son had it all planned. They knew Jesus would need to sacrifice His life to forgive our sins and bring us back into a relationship with God. The 25 fulfilled prophecies show what Jesus went through for us voluntarily. It's incredible! It's simple and clear: God loves you!

   "But God demonstrates his own love for us in this: While we were still sinners, Christ died for us" **(Romans 5:8).**

Dear Jesus:

_____

_____

_____

Jesus with skin on:

Beyond Star Wars

"The resurrection of Jesus Christ ranks as history's most revolutionary event." [10]
—Bill Bright

C hecking It Out

"The force be with you." In the movie *Star Wars: A New Hope*, when Obi-Wan Kenobi completes Luke Skywalker's training to defeat Darth Vader, the cosmic battle of good versus evil is on. With that statement, Luke had a new, supernatural power that took him beyond his own ability. From that point, it was clear that, in the battles and struggles he encountered, good would win—Darth Vader and the forces of evil would be defeated.

That was only a movie, or several of them. But what about reality? Is there a real Force that will be with us? Yes, but it is a far different Force than what is portrayed in the *Star Wars* series. The real Force is the resurrection of Jesus Christ. Rooted in history, proven fact and reality, it is the dynamic spiritual force that changes people's lives, changes the world and, ultimately will cause God to win over evil. Without it, people just exist. With it, they can really live!

Without it, the apostle Paul says,

"And if Christ has not been raised, our preaching is useless and so is your faith. . . . But Christ has indeed been raised from the dead"
(1 Corinthians 15:14, 20).

But with it:

"But thanks be to God! He gives us the victory through our Lord Jesus Christ" (1 Corinthians 15:57).

Hot Notes:

G etting the Point

What an important event! Did it really happen? Before you finish this book, you will have all kinds of information to answer that question. But right now, let's see if the Old Testament prophets thought it would happen. They viewed the resurrection of the Messiah from four different angles. All of them together formed a beautiful picture of what would take place when Jesus rose from the dead.

1. His Resurrection

The resurrection means the event when Jesus was raised from the dead.

"Therefore my heart is glad and my tongue rejoices; my body also will rest secure, because you will not abandon me to the grave, nor will you let your Holy One see decay" (Psalm 16:9, 10).

"After two days he will revive us; on the third day he will restore us, that we may live in his presence" (Hosea 6:2).

Other verses on the resurrection of the Messiah include Psalm 30:3; 41:10; 118:17.

2. His Ascension

The ascension means the event when Jesus ascended into Heaven forty days after the resurrection.

"When you ascended on high, you led captives in your train; you received gifts from men, even from the rebellious—that you, O Lord God, might dwell there" (Psalm 68:18).

Other verses on the ascension of the Messiah include Psalm 16:11; 24:7; 110:1; 118:19.

3. His Second Coming (Second Advent)

The second coming means the event when Jesus will come back to earth and judge it.

"For to us a child is born, to us a son is given, and the government will be on his shoulders. . . . He will reign on David's throne and over his kingdom, establishing and upholding it with justice and righteousness from that time on and forever. The zeal of the Lord Almighty will accomplish this" (Isaiah 9:6, 7).

Other verses on the second coming of the Messiah are Psalm 50:3-6; Isaiah 66:18; Zechariah 14:4-9.

4. His Reign

The reign of the Messiah means that period after the second coming when He will rule over the earth and then reign as King of kings and Lord of lords throughout eternity.

"In my vision at night I looked, and there before me was one like a son of man, coming with the clouds of heaven. He approached the Ancient of Days and was led into his presence. He was given authority, glory and sovereign power; all peoples, nations and men of every language worshiped him. His dominion is an everlasting dominion that will not pass away, and his kingdom is one that will never be destroyed" (Daniel 7:13, 14).

Other verses on the reign of the Messiah include 1 Chronicles 17:11-14; Psalm 2:6-8; 8:6; 45:6, 7; 72:8; 110:1-3.

In these four ways the prophets foretold what would happen at Jesus' resurrection and beyond. That's way beyond *Star Wars!*

Heavy Thoughts:

Looking Inside

If Jesus did not rise from the dead, then He has no validity or reality for us today. He would simply be a dead Jew who left a nice religion. But if He did rise, then it is the most amazing event in all of history. And it offers us the answers to life's most searching issues: Who am I? Where am I going? How am I going to get there? Then we know that God exists, what He is like and how we may know Him in our personal experience. Our lives take on meaning and purpose and it is possible to experience God in our lives every day.[11]

Even beyond that, we have the personal power to live the Christian life because we have the resurrection power of Jesus living in us through the Holy Spirit. That makes what Jesus did in history extremely real for us today!

Jesus said, **"I am the resurrection and the life. He who believes in me will live, even though he dies; and whoever lives and believes in me will never die. Do you believe this?" (John 11:25, 26).**

Dear Jesus:

Jesus with skin on:

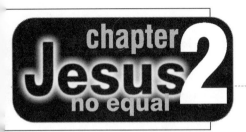

Down to Earth

I'm a killer. I don't want to be, but I can't help it. Almost without realizing it, I bring destruction and death to an innocent, peace-loving family.

Here's the situation: The pavement in my driveway has some cracks in it. Some ants have built their homes under the concrete slab. I see them crawling in and out over the ridge of dirt they've built up around the entrance to their subdivision.

It's not a pretty sight when I back out of the driveway. I look back to see all of these little guys strewn across the pavement. They've been crunched. A few have gotten caught in between the tire treads and they are hanging on for dear life. The rest of the survivors frantically zigzag back and forth. They have no idea what hit them. The thought occurs that I could call the ant paramedics. On second thought, I could try yelling at the little critters: "Avoid the pain! Move your house three feet to the left!" But the fact is, I'll never be able to communicate with those ants.

The only way I could make them understand would be for me to become one of them.

That's exactly what Jesus did!

Camping Out

Jesus came to earth because He wanted to communicate with us on a level we could understand. John, the disciple of Jesus, zeros in on how Jesus came to communicate with us. *"The Word became flesh and made his dwelling among us. We have seen his glory, the glory of the One and Only, who came from the Father, full of grace and truth"* (John 1:14).

When John used the words *"made his dwelling among us"* he meant literally, "pitched his tent." Imagine that! God sent Jesus to pitch His tent with us so we could get to know Him. He camped out with us because He wanted to communicate with us about who He is, who we are and how we relate to Him.

So what did Jesus do while He was hiking and camping on this earth? In his letter to the Galatian Christians, the apostle Paul explains what He did: *"But when the time had fully come, God sent his Son, born of a woman, born under law, to redeem those under law, that we might receive the full rights of sons. Because you are sons, God sent the Spirit of his Son into our hearts, the Spirit who calls out, 'Abba, Father.' So you are no longer a slave, but a son; and since you are a son, God has made you also an heir"* (Galatians 4:4-7).

We find here three "down to earth" expressions of what God did in Christ, three significant ways God camped out with us in Jesus:
- He came to a cradle (v. 4—He was born of a woman).
- He carried a cross (v. 5—He redeemed us).
- He captured a crown (vv. 6, 7—He made us sons and heirs).

A Cradle

Excitement filled the house. We had known for nine months that we were going to have a baby. Now the time had arrived. We left the house for the hospital in the morning. At four o'clock in the afternoon, the nurses wheeled Carol into the delivery room. We had decided that if the baby was a girl, we would call her "Katie." If we had a boy, his name would be "Scott." (We had confidence it would be one or the other!) Carol worked really hard at bringing that baby into the world. Suddenly the nurse began to yell, "It's a Scott! It's a Scott!"

What is she talking about? Then it hit me. I'm a father! I have a Scott! (Later we had a Katie, then a Jonathan, and, fourteen years after Scott we had a Ginny!)

That's how exciting it must have been when Jesus was born, right? Wrong. A tired young mother-to-be, probably still a teenager, made an exhausting journey to Bethlehem from Nazareth and arrived in the overcrowded, dusty town just when her baby was due.

Imagine Joseph and Mary—a young couple engaged to be married—who find out that Mary is pregnant. On top of having a baby out of wedlock, Joseph is not even the father. Joseph loved Mary, and, gentleman that he was, decided to break up with Mary quietly. That is, until God sent a messenger to tell Joseph that the child had been conceived (get this!) by the Holy Spirit (Matthew 1:18-21).

Adding to the trauma, they had to go to Bethlehem from Nazareth for a census. That meant they had to travel miles on donkeyback. But they had no choice. The Roman government demanded that they go.

That night when they arrived in Bethlehem, it looked like the halls of your school when classes change—wall-to-wall people. The place was a madhouse. Joseph tried to find a room—quickly! He knew that Mary was ready to deliver the baby at any time. He was told at every place, "NO VACANCY." When he tried to explain to one innkeeper that the baby was on the way, the best the innkeeper could do was let Joseph use his stable, probably a cave behind his inn.

Do you get the picture? No new baby bed or furniture. No freshly painted room. No Pampers. No sterile hospital with doctors and nurses. Nothing but a cold, smelly, dirty stable. With perhaps only a few animals to watch, Jesus Christ was born. If God had not announced the occasion to some shepherds in the fields nearby, no human being besides His parents would have noticed the tiny, wiggling form that Mary wrapped in a cloth and placed in a feed trough. What a way for the Son of God to enter the world!

Imagine Mary, exhausted and cold, caressing the tiny hands of her nursing child—hands that one day would reach out and touch blind men's eyes and make them see. In that dark, cold cave that night, the tiny feet that would one day walk the hills of Galilee kicked softly in the manger straw. They were the same feet that one day would turn toward Jerusalem and face death on a cross.

The squeaky noises from Jesus' mouth expressed the first earthly sounds of the One who would one day say, *"I am the way and the truth and the life. No one comes to the Father except through me"* (John 14:6).

This tiny baby, wrapped in a blanket in a manger, was God's Son—the link between a loving Father and a lost world. God became a man. For what purpose? To communicate God's love to people like you and me who could never understand it in any other way.

What does that cradle mean to us?

The same God who brought about the miracle of Jesus' birth wants every person to experience a new birth. "I've already been born!" you say. Naturally! Once! But Jesus says we need to be born a second time, supernaturally. He tells us we need to be born spiritually just as we were born physically. Check out what He said. Once a man named Nicodemus asked Jesus how to have eternal life. Jesus replied, *"I tell you the truth, no one can see the kingdom of God unless he is born again"* (John 3:3).

When a person experiences spiritual birth, that person's life is changed. No way your life is going to stay the same! Let's get this straight. When a person is born again, it does not mean joining a church, becoming part of a youth group, going through confirmation classes or catechism, "turning over a new leaf" or becoming religious.

What it does mean is LIFE! When Jesus told Nicodemus that he needed to be born again, He was talking about entering into a dynamic, personal relationship with the living God—inviting Jesus to enter into a person's life and take control, changing it from the inside out. Once that happens, that person will never be the same again.

John said it well: *"Yet to all who received him, to those who believed in his name, he gave the right to become children of God—children born not of natural descent, nor of human decision . . . but born of God"* (John 1:12, 13). A person is born again when he or she receives Jesus into his or her life.

Jesus said it best: *"Here I am! I stand at the door and knock. If anyone hears my voice and opens the door, I will come in and eat with him, and he with me"* (Revelation 3:20).

Jesus stands at the door of each person's life and knocks. In fact, He stands at the door of your life and knocks. If you let Him live inside you, you are born again. If you don't open the door of your life, then you are not born again. It's that simple.

Understand that Jesus won't beat the door down. He responds to you as a gentleman. If you don't want to open the door, that is your choice. But if you do open it, He promises to come in. And when He does, you have LIFE!

A Cross

"Randy," I asked, "suppose someone came along and kidnapped your girlfriend, Susan, then sent you a note saying if you paid so much money, she would be set free. How much would you pay to get her back? Ten dollars?"

"Sure," Randy said.

"What about $25?"

"Yeah, sure."

"What about $100? $500? $1000? How about a million?"

"Sure, if I could get hold of that much, I'd pay a million," Randy replied.

In an even bigger ransom deal, the apostle Paul wrote, *"But when the time had fully come, God sent his Son, born of a woman, born under law, to redeem those under law, that we might receive the full rights of sons"* (Galatians 4:4, 5).

"Redeem" means to buy back, to make an exchange for something you consider of great value. Paying the ransom, as Randy was willing to do to get Susan back from the kidnappers, gives us the idea expressed in the word redeem.

Mankind was captured by sin and was headed straight to Hell—to be eternally separated from the love and presence of God. But Christ came to buy us back. And what a price He paid! If we want to know how much God was willing to pay to redeem us—to buy us back, all we have to do is look at Jesus on the cross.

Imagine the agony and pain in God's heart as He and Jesus counseled in Heaven over man's condition. Imagine the Father's anguish when He decided what the price would be—that His only Son should come to earth to be spat on, beaten, mistreated, scourged, mocked and nailed to a cross.

My wife Carol and I were blessed with four children. I love them dearly. I also love teenagers. I'm glad no one has ever asked me to give the life of one of my children so that another teenager could live. I love students, but none of them means so much to me that I would offer my own child to die for them.

Maybe that gives us some idea of the depth of the love God has for us. He willingly gave His only Son to die for us so that we might be bought back—and brought back—to Him. He loved us that much. If we can see how much God loves us, as He demonstrated on the cross, then instead of living as though Jesus never died, we will want to live for Him.

How do we live because of what Christ did on the cross?

How do we then live in light of the fact that Jesus paid the price to buy us back with His own life?

The apostle Paul gives us a cool clue: *"And so, dear brothers and sisters, I plead with you to give your bodies to God. Let them be a living and holy sacrifice—the kind he will accept. When you think of what he has done for you, is this too much to ask?"* (Romans 12:1, NLT).

The same word that is used here of Christ's sacrifice is used of our sacrifice. Jesus died on the cross for us. He wants us, in turn, to die to ourselves. What does it mean to "die to ourselves"? To answer that question, we must ask what it is within each of us that raises its ugly head and says, "I will do it my way!" What is it? Your temper? A bad attitude toward your parents? Selfishness? A desire for attention? An addiction to "your stuff"? Impure sexual desires? Hurt and bitter feelings? Those things we need to die to.

To do that, Jesus asks that we offer ourselves—the good, the bad and the ugly—to Him. Instead of "I will do it my way," Jesus wants to do it *His* way. When we get so sick of ourselves that we want to die to ourselves, then He will live through us.

A Crown

Imagine getting everything you want and as much as you want: 500 new CDs, 100 new shirts, 50 pairs of jeans and ten new sports cars. That's what it would be like if you were the son or daughter of a king. And you are! You get to wear the crown.

God calls us believers His children—sons and daughters. Check out Galatians 4:6, 7: *"Because you are sons, God sent the Spirit of his Son into our hearts, the Spirit who calls out, 'Abba, Father.' So you are no longer a slave, but a son; and since you are a son, God has made you also an heir."* Even though God does not give us all of our material wants, because He knows that's not good for us, He has promised to give us everything we need because we are His sons and daughters.

Doug was a kid who lived next door to us. He came over a lot. Once he came over and said, "Hey, Barry, will you give me a dollar?" What did I say? Depending on what mood I was in, I'd probably say, "Go home. Don't be a jerk. Ask your own dad for a dollar. You're not my son."

I have a son named Jonathan. What if he came to me and said, "Dad, can I have a dollar?" What would I say then? "Okay, here, son. Take it." I give the money to him because he is my son.

God says we are His kids. He wants to treat us like sons and daughters. We are His heirs—the King's kids.

As Jonathan's dad I don't give him everything he asks for. I know he doesn't need some of it. And I know some of it wouldn't be good for him. In the same way, God knows that some of the things we ask for aren't really needed or they aren't good for us. And wisely, He withholds these things. But God the Father has given us everything we will ever need in Jesus Christ.

God gave us something far more valuable than I could ever give my son. He put our names in the will of His Son, Jesus. We are God's heirs. When Jesus died, all that He had became ours. We get to wear the crown! The apostle Paul expressed it like this: *"How we praise God, the Father of our Lord Jesus Christ, who has blessed us with every spiritual blessing in the heavenly realms because we belong to Christ"* (Ephesians 1:3, NLT).

The apostle Peter told us that when we wear the crown, *"His divine power has given us everything we need for life and godliness"* (2 Peter 1:3).

Probably the best statement comes from Romans 8:16, 17: *"For his Holy Spirit speaks to us deep in our hearts and tells us that we are God's children. And since we are his children, we will share his treasures—for everything God gives to his Son, Christ, is ours, too. But if we are to share his glory, we must also share his suffering"* (NLT). We get to wear the crown!

Why did He come? Jesus came in human form to identify with us. And He gave His life on the cross to redeem us, so that we could inherit everything we need to live for Him. Sound good? It's better than you think! But remember one thing—before the crown comes the cross. And that aspect of what Jesus did merits closer examination.

Up Close and Personal

1. *When and where were you born? Ask one of your parents to describe the event to you. What are some similarities between your birth and Jesus' birth? What are some differences?*

2. *Look over John 3:1-8 and describe what you think it means to be "born again."*

3. *Using what you learned on page 35 about the word "redeem," express what it means to you that Jesus redeemed you when He died on the cross.*

4. *As a believer, you are a child of God. What does God give you as His child? (See Romans 8:16, 17; Galatians 4:6, 7; Ephesians 1:3-14; 2 Peter 1:3, 4.)*

5. *How do you like the idea of sharing the inheritance of the great King of the universe? Take a few minutes to reflect on (and write down) what that means to you.*

The Birth of Jesus

day 1 Visit to Planet Earth

"He was born of earthly parentage. Though He was God, He became a man. He was the Ancient of Days, yet He was born at a point in time. He created worlds and companied with celestial beings, yet He came to live in a family setting on earth."[1]
—Henry Gariepy

Checking It Out

Oxymorons. We use them to try to describe unusual phenomena, things like jumbo shrimp, sweet and sour sauce, pretty ugly and awfully beautiful. They are difficult to explain. Like, why do we make hot tea then put ice in it, and why do we make sweet tea and then put lemon in it? It doesn't really make sense.

Life is filled with contradictory realities. The incarnation of God in the person of Jesus Christ is an incredibly complex oxymoron: The infinite God in a finite person. No way to explain that. It's a mystery. How could God become fully man? How could a man be fully God? The apostle John gave the best explanation. What do you think he is saying about Jesus being fully God/fully man?

"In the beginning was the Word, and the Word was with God, and the Word was God. He was with God in the beginning. Through him all things were made; without him nothing was made that has been made. In him was life, and that life was the light of men. The light shines in the darkness, but the darkness has not understood it. . . . The Word became flesh and made his dwelling among us. We have seen his glory, the glory of the One and Only, who came from the Father, full of grace and truth" (John 1:1-5, 14).

Hot Notes:

Getting the Point

Often people get confused when they try to figure out who Jesus really is. Is He God? Or is He man?

He was born in the flesh. Mary gave birth to Him. He lived in time. He grew up in a real place. Yet the Bible teaches that He existed from the beginning of time. Jesus was the "incarnation" of God. Incarnation means "in the flesh." Jesus Christ is the one and only incarnation of God. He is the embodiment of God. Jesus was fully God and fully man. God visited the earth in the form of a human being, Jesus.

In John 1:1-5, 14 we discover probably the best explanation ever given of the incarnation. "The Word" is Jesus. John gives the "Top 10" descriptions of Jesus as "fully God, fully man."

1. He was in the beginning (before there was time).
2. He was with God.
3. He was God.
4. He created all things.
5. He was life.
6. He was light shining in the darkness.
7. He became flesh.
8. He lived among us.
9. He was full of grace and truth.
10. He expressed the glory of God.

Imagine that first Christmas day. Picture Jesus in the manger. What would you have seen?

- The tiny clenched hand of a baby that would someday be ruthlessly wrenched open and nailed to a Roman cross for the sin and guilt of the world.
- Hands that were too small to reach up and touch the noses of the animals, yet one day would reach out to the crowds to unstop deaf ears, open blind eyes and raise the dead.
- Eyes that were unable to follow the swishing tails or swaying heads of the animals, but one day would be able to look on the crowds of people and say "the fields are white for harvest."
- Feet not yet able to stand up, but later would stride through the corridors of the centuries shedding light on dark hearts, easing people's sorrows, taking away sin and bringing joy to life.

Heavy Thoughts:

Looking Inside

If Jesus was not fully God and fully man, then who, or what was He? When we look at Jesus Christ, we see God. He is *"the visible expression of the invisible God"* (Colossians 1:15, Phillips).

If He was God, then what does that mean for us? Jesus is with us every minute of the day wherever we are or whatever we are doing.

"The virgin will be with child and will give birth to a son, and they will call him Immanuel—which means, 'God with us'" (Matthew 1:23).

Dear Jesus:

Jesus with skin on:

An Unusual Pregnancy

"The virgin birth has never been a stumbling block in my struggle with Christianity; it is far less mind-boggling than the Power of all Creation stooping so low as to become one of us."[2]
—Madeleine L'Engle

Checking It Out

Imagine this dialogue from a teenage girl: "Bill and I had been together for fifteen months when we discovered I was pregnant. It wasn't the result of the first time we had sinned, but we had convinced ourselves it was right—right because we were in love. Naturally my first thought was marriage, but this was completely out of the question due to our ages. . . . What do we tell our parents?"

Each year about 1.1 million teenage girls in the United States become pregnant. What if that were you? Maybe it has been you! How would you feel? What would you do?

Once another girl got pregnant, but her pregnancy was totally different. In a most unusual set of circumstances she discovered she was pregnant. How was this pregnancy different?

"In the sixth month of Elizabeth's pregnancy, God sent the angel Gabriel to Nazareth, a village in Galilee, to a virgin named Mary. She was engaged to be married to a man named Joseph, a descendant of King David. Gabriel appeared to her and said, 'Greetings, favored woman! The Lord is with you!'

Confused and disturbed, Mary tried to think what the angel could mean. 'Don't be frightened, Mary,' the angel told her, 'for God has decided to bless you! You will become pregnant and have a son and you are to name him Jesus. He will be very great and will be called the Son of the Most High. And the Lord God will give him the throne of his ancestor David. And he will reign over Israel forever; his Kingdom will never end!'

Mary asked the angel, 'But how can I have a baby? I am a virgin.'

The angel replied, 'The Holy Spirit will come upon you, and the power of the Most High will overshadow you. So the baby born to you will be holy, and he will be called the Son of God.'" (Luke 1:26-35, NLT).

Hot Notes:

Getting the Point

The contrast between these two pregnancies: one is a tragedy, the other is a miracle. One person defined a miracle as "something that just can't happen until it does." Today all miracles are offensive to our scientific minds. We thumb our noses in disbelief even before we have checked out the facts. But no miracle has been as detestable as the virgin birth. The birth of Jesus violates the inviolable, breaks the unbreakable. It ranks right up there with the incarnation and the resurrection. And it did happen, the way the Bible says it did. What other explanation is there, except that Jesus was a fraud and the Bible is a book of lies?

We don't know what this teenager, Mary, was doing when the angel appeared, but the angel surprised her. To soothe her fear he gave her two encouraging words. First, he called her "favored." Instead of experiencing shame, the angel told her that God would honor her as the Messiah's mother. Secondly, he promised that whatever happened, God's presence would be with her.

Mary's response was natural. She was frightened. And the angel told her, "Don't be frightened, Mary." Then the angel Gabriel broke the news to her. He told her that she was going to have a baby. If the presence of the angel wasn't frightening enough, certainly this scared her to death. But the angel gave her specific details about what the baby would be like.

1. He will be a **son** (a boy, not a girl).
2. He will have **the name Jesus** (Joshua, which means "the one who saves").
3. He will be **very great**. (Mega is the word.)
4. He will be called **Son of the Most High**. (He is not a son, but *the* Son.)
5. He will be given **the throne of his ancestor David**. (He will reign as king.)
6. He will **reign over Israel forever**. (His rule will never end. He is eternal.)
7. He will be **born of the Holy Spirit**. (*"The Holy Spirit will come on you, and God, the Most High will overshadow you"* [Luke 1:35]—He would be conceived by the Holy Spirit, not Joseph.)
8. He will be **holy**. (He is a far cry from the illegitimate child people will think she had.)
9. He will be called the **Son of God** (the totally unique and eternal Son).

Heavy Thoughts:

Looking Inside

If we can believe this, we can believe anything! But if God is God, why not? He can have Jesus be born of a virgin and pull off the resurrection too! Why? Because *"nothing is impossible with God"* (Luke 1:37). The key here is to get our thinking on the level of God's thinking, rather than putting God in a small box with us. Think about it this way:

Every *word* of God can be believed by us, because no *work* of God is impossible for Him.

Remember, the same miracle-working Holy Spirit who came upon Mary and produced Jesus lives in you!

Dear Jesus:

Jesus with skin on:

The Revolutionary

"The Man of Nazareth has, by universal consent, been the mightiest Factor in our world's history: alike politically, socially, intellectually and morally. If He be not the Messiah, He has at least thus far done the Messiah's work. If He be not the Messiah, there has at least been none other, before or after Him. If he be not the Messiah, the world has not, and never can have a Messiah."[3]
—Alfred Edersheim

Checking It Out

It's a girl thing. Women and babies. Girls play dolls from the time they are old enough to walk. Guys are out in the dirt smashing trucks into each other. Get a group of girls together—any age—and before long the conversation is about babies. Perhaps the ultimate "girl experience" is a baby shower. I've been "a fly on the wall" at a couple of these. It's different. The conversation runs along these lines: "What do you think about this name?" "Oh, I just love this little blanket. Isn't that adorable?" "I've been working hard to get the room ready." "What other things do you need?" "Whaaaaa—the baby is kicking me a lot lately!" "What does the doctor say? Have you seen the sonogram?" And on and on it goes and when the conversation will stop, nobody knows. Why? Because girls get into those things.

Mary, Jesus' mom, was no exception. In fact, she took a trip right after she encountered the angel, to get some "girl time" with her cousin Elizabeth, who was six months pregnant already. We don't know what all went on during that time. But we do know that before she had put her suitcase down they were talking baby talk. The Bible says that when Elizabeth saw her, her baby leaped inside of her and she exclaimed in a loud voice,

"Blessed are you among women, and blessed is the child you will bear!" (Luke 1:42).

Hot Notes:

Getting the Point

Read Luke 1:39-56.

Elizabeth and Mary built each other up with positive encouragement. Both of them knew that the baby Mary was carrying was the totally unique Son of God. Then right in the middle of the conversation, Mary broke out into a spontaneous, Spirit-led song of praise. Through the years it has been known as the "Magnificat." Suddenly the tone changed. It wasn't just a girl thing anymore—it was a Spirit thing—and a revolutionary one at that. Check out what this teenage girl had to say:

1. Mary turned the focus from herself to God.
* God is the Lord (v. 46). He is the ruler of the world and of her life.
* God is the Savior (v. 47). She calls him "my Savior." He has come to save the people from themselves and their sins.
* God is mighty (v. 49). The God who made Heaven and Earth makes this great thing happen to Mary.

- God is holy (v. 49). He is in a class all by Himself. No one else compares to Him.
- God is merciful (v. 50). He has compassion on those who are helpless and in distress. Nowhere has His mercy been displayed more clearly than in sending His only Son to rescue us.
- God is powerful (v. 51). When He flexes His muscles, the whole earth reverberates. With His power, He starts a revolution.

2. Mary told about an astounding revolution that was about to begin.

In reading the text it sounds like Mary continues to recite God's wonderful actions. But, in the original Greek text, the tense here switches to indicate that these actions are in the future rather than in the past (and you thought English class was tough!).

One man called the Magnificat "the most revolutionary document in the world." That's because it tells us about three revolutions that God is going to bring about through this baby Messiah:

• A moral revolution (v. 51)

God will scatter the proud. He will take their arrogant plans that they have devised in their hearts, crumble them and then toss them to the wind. Jesus deals a crushing blow to pride. When we see ourselves compared to Jesus, we see our sin, rather than how good we think we are, and we stand in the floodlight of shame. Jesus helps us see ourselves the way we are, then changes us.

• A social revolution (v. 52)

He will bring down rulers from their thrones and will lift up the humble. When we realize what Christ has done for us, then all the ground is level at the foot of the cross. He puts an end to cliques, prestige and labeling other people by their differences from us.

• An economic revolution (v. 53)

He will fill the hungry with good things, and the rich will walk away with empty hands. Without Christ, our desire is to "get all we can; can all we get; and sit on the can." But where Jesus is present, no one wants to have too much while others have too little. With Jesus, we get in order to give it away.[4]

When Jesus came on the scene, the sweet loveliness of the baby shower took a radical turn to a people-changing, world-changing revolution.

Heavy Thoughts:

Looking Inside

Mary described the revolution that Jesus will bring and has now brought. These words come from a teenager just like you. She could talk about and live out that revolution because she knew God intimately.

As you spend time with God, what is He saying to you about what you need to do to join the revolution? How does He want to use you to bring about a radical revolution in your life and in the lives of those around you?

Don't mess around. Grab hold of it and go!

"From the days of John the Baptist until now, the kingdom of heaven has been forcefully advancing, and forceful men [people] lay hold of it" (Matthew 11:12).

Dear Jesus:

Jesus with skin on:

"The God who roared, who could order armies and empires about like pawns on a chessboard, this God emerged in Palestine as a baby who could not speak or eat solid food or control his bladder, who depended on a teenager for shelter, food, and love."[5]
—*Philip Yancey*

Checking It Out

When it was time for the baby's delivery, I took my wife Carol to the car and drove her to the hospital. I pulled up to the door and they placed her in a wheelchair. She checked into a nice room. The nurses came in and took all of her vital signs. They prepped her for delivery. Then they stood by ready to meet every need. When it was time, the doctor came in and with maximal effort by Carol and minimal effort by the doctor (and me), the baby emerged. The nurse yelled: "It's a Scott!" Having a baby is not exactly in the fun category for the mother, but the hospital provided every convenience to make it as pleasant as possible.

Contrast that with the following birth account. Look for all the ways Jesus' birth was a difficult experience for Mary and Joseph.

"At the time the Roman emperor, Augustus, decreed that a census should be taken throughout the Roman Empire. (This was the first census taken when Quirinius was governor of Syria.) All returned to their own towns to register for this census. And because Joseph was a descendant of King David, he had to go to Bethlehem in Judea, David's ancient home. He traveled there from the village of Nazareth in Galilee. He took with him Mary, his fiancée, who was obviously pregnant by this time. And while they were there, the time came for her baby to be born. She gave birth to her first child, a son. She wrapped him snugly in strips of cloth and laid him in a manger, because there was no room for them in the village inn"
(Luke 2:1-7, NLT).

Hot Notes:

Getting the Point

This story tells of the birth of Jesus simply and clearly. Three facts show us how special this particular birth was compared to all others.

1. God had the delivery of the baby timed perfectly.

Several factors make the timing of Jesus' birth perfect.

- "At that time" Caesar and Rome ruled the whole world. They controlled from Britain and Spain to the Caspian Sea (now Russia). Because the entire world was under one government with one transportation system and one communication system, the message of Jesus was able to spread to the whole world in a brief amount of time.
- Jesus' birth occurred when "Augustus decreed that a census should be taken." This kind of census was taken every fourteen years primarily to get information and assess taxes. This one was taken in 8 B.C., the year Jesus was born.
- "Quirinius was governor of Syria" at the time of Jesus' birth. He was governor twice—from 10 B.C. to 7 B.C. and again in 6 A.D. This was the first census taken while he was governor, which means it had to be during his first term. This shows us that Jesus was born in 8 B.C.

Look at how God orchestrated the events for Jesus to be born *"when the time had fully come"* (Galatians 4:4). THE TIMING WAS PERFECT!

2. God had the place of the birth designed perfectly.

Jesus' birth took place when everyone returned to their own towns to register for this census. That means that Mary and Joseph had to travel from their home in Nazareth to Bethlehem, an 80-mile trip.

Why did the emperor have a census? To show how powerful he was. He did it for pride and power. But God had a bigger purpose. He orchestrated the event so that the whole world would be taxed. That way he could transport Mary and Joseph from Nazareth to Bethlehem—to the right place to have the baby. Their presence there fulfilled the prophecy of Micah 5:2 that Jesus would be born in Bethlehem.

Do you see how God arranged the events to get Mary and Joseph to the right place? THE PLACE WAS PERFECT!

3. God allowed the difficult circumstances to accomplish His plan.

Joseph didn't want to leave Mary in Nazareth for several reasons:

- She had already been with her cousin Elizabeth for three months. That's a long time to be apart when two people are in love.
- To leave her would expose her to gossip about the baby. They could even stone her for having a baby outside of marriage (see Leviticus 20:10).
- He wanted to be with her. He knew what a special child this was.

But this was a difficult trip. Can you begin to imagine how unbelievably tired Mary must have felt—being nine months pregnant and riding a donkey for 80 miles?

Then, when they finally arrived, "No Vacancy" was posted at every inn. So they bedded down probably in a cave where animals were kept—a stable. When the baby came, the only place to put Jesus was not in a nice baby bed, but a manger, which literally means "a place where animals feed." She wrapped him in a piece of cloth that could have been her own scarf.

The circumstances looked far from ideal, but God, who wanted to identify with the poorest human beings, made the environment just right. THE CIRCUMSTANCES WERE PERFECT!

God was carrying out His perfect plan; Mary and Joseph knew it.

"She looks into the face of the baby. Her son. Her Lord. His Majesty. At this point in history, the human being who best understands who God is and what he is doing is a teenage girl in a smelly stable. She can't take her eyes off him. Somehow Mary knows she is holding God. So this is he. She remembers the words of the angel. 'His kingdom will never end.'

He looks like anything but a king. His face is prunish and red. His cry, though strong and healthy, is still the helpless and piercing cry of a baby. And he is absolutely dependent upon Mary for his well-being.

Majesty in the midst of the mundane. Holiness in the filth of sheep manure and sweat. Divinity entering the world on the floor of a stable, through the womb of a teenager and in the presence of a carpenter."[6]

Heavy Thoughts:

Looking Inside

God's timing, place and circumstances, as difficult as they were, were absolutely perfect in bringing Jesus into the world.

Has He given the same careful planning to your life? Did He put you here at the right time? Do you live in the right place, even if you don't like it? Even though your circumstances are difficult, are they right for you now?

God made you a promise that His plan for you is as perfect as the one He had for Jesus!

"'For I know the plans I have for you,' declares the LORD, 'plans to prosper you and not to harm you, plans to give you hope and a future'" (Jeremiah 29:11).

Dear Jesus:

Jesus with skin on:

It's Party Time!

"Hark! the herald angels sing, 'Glory to the newborn King;
Peace on earth and mercy mild, God and sinners reconciled!'
Joyful, all ye nations, rise, join the triumph of the skies;
With the angelic host proclaim, 'Christ is born in Bethlehem!'"
—"Hark the Herald Angels," by John Wesley

Checking It Out

A six-year-old boy had a part in the Christmas pageant. He had practiced and practiced his one line: "For behold I bring you good tidings of great joy which shall be to all people." On the night of the pageant he was nervous. When it came time for his line, he forgot it. In desperation he blurted out, "Man, have I got good news for you!"

That cuts through it all and gets us to the bottom line. The birth of Jesus is a celebration—a party— because it brought good news. That's what the angel said:

"Don't be afraid! . . . I bring you good news of great joy for everyone! The Savior—yes, the Messiah, the Lord—has been born tonight in Bethlehem, the city of David" (Luke 2:10, 11, NLT)

Hot Notes:

Getting the Point

Read Luke 2:8-20. A whole bunch of people were invited to the party. Each group was invited for a reason.

The Shepherds

The shepherds got a special invitation—an angel invited them. That probably scared them to death. Imagine camping out by the fire and suddenly a creature from another world—an angel—appears in a bright light.

The shepherds couldn't believe they got invited. They didn't deserve to go. They were despised by the religious people because they didn't keep all the legalistic rules. They were considered low class, not worthy, and besides—they were smelly from hanging around sheep all the time.

But they got invited because they kept special sheep. In the temple in Jerusalem the Jewish people offered an unblemished lamb to God every morning and evening to take away the people's sins. To make sure they were unblemished, the Jewish leaders had their own private flock near Bethlehem.

How interesting that God invited the shepherds who watched after the lambs who took away the sins. Now they got to be the first ones to see *"the Lamb of God, who takes away the sin of the world"* (John 1:29).

The Angel and All His Heavenly Friends

A message always has to have a messenger. In this case God used an angel. He brought the good news: the Savior, the Messiah, the Lord had been born that night in Bethlehem.

He brought with him all of his buddies—an army of angels. They were singing at the top of their lungs: *"Glory to God in the highest, and on earth peace to men on whom his favor rests"* (Luke 2:14).

That was really important because in those days when a baby was born, the local band came to the house to sing. Since Jesus was in a stable 80 miles away from home, God put together a special choir just for Him! Now the shepherds were really blown away.

After a few songs the shepherds got into the party mood. They said, *"Let's go to Bethlehem and see this thing that has happened, which the Lord has told us about"* (Luke 2:15). And they did!

The Baby and His Family

The baby was the reason for the party—the star of the show. Why all the fuss over one little baby in a dumpy little manger? Who was He, anyway? Luke 2:11, 12 gives us a clear description of Him:

- He is the **Savior**.

  That means that He has come to save them from sin and death and to give them life.
- He is the **Christ**.

  He came as the Anointed One, the Messiah, the One who fulfills all the promises of God.
- He is the **Lord**.

  He rules and reigns over all the earth and has power and authority over people's lives.

All this wrapped up in one little baby. Right here we see the ultimate genius of God. He brought forth a baby, wrapped in strips of cloth and lying in a manger. That little baby is *"the Savior, Christ the Lord!"*

Heavy Thoughts:

Looking Inside

The baby Jesus—before He could even talk—had already touched the lives of the lowest (the shepherds) and the highest (the angels). Whether you're a scumbag or a perfect angel, Jesus wants to invite you to the party. It's not about being religious or going to church. It's about you doing what the shepherds did when they said, "Come on, let's go." And they went to get to know Jesus. How did they get there? The same way you do.

- *Take your invitation. (You have one now.)*
- *Run to Jesus.*
- *Spend time with Him.*
- *Tell everyone you meet.*

Dear Jesus:

Jesus with skin on:

Two Witnesses

"Maker of the sun, He is made under the sun.
In the Father He remains, from His mother he goes forth.
Creator of heaven and earth, He was born on earth under heaven.
Unspeakably wise, He is wisely speechless.
Filling the world, He lies in a manger.
Ruler of the stars, He nurses at his mother's bosom.
He is both great in the nature of God, and small in the form of a servant."
—St. Augustine of Hippo

Checking It Out

A big Lincoln Continental smashed into my daughter's little car. It was not a pretty sight. The little Sunbird landed upside down, down the street, almost in the kitchen of a local restaurant, totaled. Nobody was killed or even badly injured, but we had to go to court. When that day came, the judge had summoned the witnesses to the court to tell what they had seen. The witnesses verified the evidence. From the evidence and the testimony of the witnesses the judge made a decision in the case.

We lost our case, but in the case of Jesus' birth, He won. In His day, if a person wanted to confirm the truth about anything, he brought forth not just one witness, but two. The two witnesses in agreement confirmed the truth of any given situation—either in or out of court.

That's where Simeon and Anna enter the picture. These two witnesses affirmed the miraculous nature of Jesus' birth and the fact that He was the Messiah.

Witness number one was Simeon.

"It had been revealed to him by the Holy Spirit that he would not die before he had seen the Lord's Christ. Moved by the Spirit, he went into the temple courts" (Luke 2:26, 27).

Witness number two was Anna, a prophetess.

"She never left the temple but worshiped night and day, fasting and praying. Coming up to them at that very moment, she gave thanks to God and spoke about the child to all who were looking forward to the redemption of Jerusalem" (Luke 2:37, 38).

Hot Notes:

Getting the Point

Read the whole account in Luke 2:21-40.

For Jesus to be a normal Jewish boy, His parents had to go through three ceremonies:

• Circumcision

Eight days after Jesus was born, His parents took Him to be circumcised. In that ceremony a boy received his name. They had no problem with that since an angel had given the name Jesus nine months before.

• The Redemption of the Firstborn

Because God had given life and every child belonged to God, this ceremony allowed parents to buy their firstborn child back from God for five coins. The parents promised to raise the child in God's service.

• The Purification of Childbirth

For forty days after childbirth a woman was considered unclean. At the end of that time, she would bring a sacrifice and offer it to God to purify herself.

Mary and Joseph, being good Jews, did all three of these. While they were in the temple in Jerusalem doing these things, they encountered the two witnesses—Simeon and Anna.

Simeon had several qualities about him that make him a viable witness (Luke 2:25).

• Righteous

He had a right relationship with God.

• Devout

He was pursuing God totally.

• Filled with the Holy Spirit

He had the Spirit of God living inside him.

• Waiting for the Messiah

Unlike most who believed that the Messiah would rule the world with military power, Simeon was known as one of the "quiet in the land." They had no dreams of powerful armies, but saw the Messiah coming to save and comfort His people.

The reason God chose Simeon as a witness was because he was looking for the right kind of Messiah. God had given this old man a promise that he would not die before he had seen the Messiah.

When he took the baby in his arms, he spoke a beautiful hymn that confirmed who Jesus was (Luke 2:28-32):

- Jesus is the **Savior.** He came to save "all people" from their sins.
- He is a **light.** He will bring the light that will reveal to all nations who God really is.
- He is the **glory.** Jesus will show the glory of God to His people Israel and will be the glory of Israel. Producing the Messiah will be Israel's crowning accomplishment.

Then when speaking to and blessing Mary and Joseph, he told four more revealing facts about the Messiah (Luke 2:33-35):

- Jesus will cause people to "rise and fall." He is the dividing point of history and for each individual. Those who reject Him will "fall." They will not experience salvation. Many will reject Him. Those who choose to follow Him will "rise." They will enter into salvation. Many will accept Him.
- Jesus will be a *"sign that will be spoken against."* Simply, this meant that Jesus' life would be

like a signpost pointing people to the character, words and actions of God.

- Jesus will *"reveal the thoughts of many hearts."* All people's true motives will be revealed when they encounter Jesus.
- Jesus will bring great pain to His mother. Simeon told Mary, *"a sword will pierce your soul."* That sword was the death of Jesus on the cross. Words could not begin to describe the hurt she would feel as a result of His suffering. The road to the cross begins with Simeon's prophecy. Simeon's message gives us a true picture, an honest testimony, a powerful witness to who Jesus really is.

Anna was an 84-year-old woman whose whole life had been centered around God. She stayed in the temple day and night, worshiping God with fasting and prayer. The Jews counted only seven prophetesses in their entire history, so this was no ordinary woman. Who better to serve as the second witness?

Her timing was perfect. She came along just as Simeon was speaking to Mary and Joseph. When she heard what he said, she began to praise God, confirming that what Simeon had said was true. She talked about Jesus to everyone who was waiting on the Messiah.

Anna, this amazing woman, joined Simeon in confirming that the Baby really was who the angels, shepherds, wise men and Mary and Joseph said He was.

Heavy Thoughts:

Looking Inside

What stands out about Simeon and Anna is that their lives made them credible witnesses to the Messiah.

What about you? Is there anything in your life that keeps you from being a credible witness?

And they didn't just live the life, they *"talked about Jesus to everyone . . ."* (Luke 2:38, NLT). *Would you say that's true of you? What one step can you take to talk more about Jesus to your friends?*

"But you will receive power when the Holy Spirit comes on you, and you will be my witnesses in Jerusalem, and in all Judea and Samaria, and to the ends of the earth" (Acts 1:8).

Dear Jesus:

Jesus with skin on:

"Jesus endured a human birth to give us a new spiritual birth. He occupied a stable that we might occupy a mansion. He had an earthly mother so that we might have a heavenly Father. He became a subject that we might be free. He left His glory to give us glory. He was poor that we might be rich. He was welcomed by shepherds at His birth whereas we at our birth are welcomed by angels. He was hunted by Herod that we might be delivered from the grasp of Satan. That is the great paradox of the Christmas story. It is that which makes it irresistibly attractive. It is the reversal of roles at God's cost for our benefit."[7]
—James Montgomery Boice

Checking It Out

Our family has a game we call "Jinx Up." To play, three people sit on one side of a big table. Three sit on the other side. One side gets a penny. They put their hands under the table and pass the penny from person to person until the other side calls "Jinx Up." Then everyone puts their elbows on the table with their hands in a fist. When the other side says "Jinx Down" everyone slams their hands down on the table trying to disguise the sound of the penny hitting the table under someone's hand. Then the other side has to guess, hand by hand, which hand has the penny under it. The trick is to choose the correct hand. If that team does, they win. If the other team disguises the sound of the penny, they win. The competition can get pretty heated.

Like trying to choose the "Jinx Up" hand with the penny, we have several options to choose from in answering the question:

"What do you think about Christ? Whose son is he?" (Matthew 22:41).

1. Illegitimate son

The rumors must have spread from His childhood days in Nazareth, because the religious leaders twisted the story of His birth to imply that He was an illegitimate child. Mocking Jesus, they say, *"We [emphatic, pointing back to Jesus] were not born out of wedlock!"* (John 8:41, NLT).

2. Joseph's son

Others knew Him growing up and they knew Joseph, His earthly father. But when He claimed to be the Messiah, they didn't believe Him. Their response was, *"Isn't this Joseph's son?"* (Luke 4:22).

3. God's Son

His Heavenly Father had a different view. When John the Baptist baptized Jesus, a voice came out of Heaven and said, *"This is my Son, whom I love; with him I am well pleased"* (Matthew 3:17).

Those are the options. Jinx up!

Hot Notes:

Getting the Point

Read these verses again: Matthew 22:41; John 8:41; Luke 4:22; Matthew 3:17.
Jinx down. Choose carefully.

Option number one:
Illegitimate son

Is it possible that Jesus' birth is not what the Bible says it is? Many scholars have tried to explain away the virgin birth. They call it a fable, a story. Down through the centuries people have constantly attacked the virgin birth. After the resurrection, it is the most attacked doctrine of the Christian faith. It has been labeled with words like "irrelevant," "questionable" and "not that important."

Option number two:
Joseph's son

Could Jesus have been just a good, moral teacher? Sure, He meant well, and He was sincere, but was He the divine Son of God? Maybe just Joseph's son?

What makes people think He was Joseph's son and nothing more?

- The genealogies of Jesus in Matthew 1:1-17 and Luke 3:23-38 both trace the genealogy of Jesus through Joseph. That seems strange if Joseph is not His real father.
- The name "father" is used of Joseph when he was searching for Jesus in the temple (Luke 2:48). Jesus is referred to as Joseph's son on several other occasions (see Matthew 13:55 and John 6:42).
- The rest of the New Testament says virtually nothing about the virgin birth.

With those reasons in one hand, in the other hand grab a couple of simple observations that argue that Jesus was more than Joseph's son.

- The Old Testament said the virgin birth (actually virgin conception) would happen—Isaiah 7:14.
- When we read the stories of Jesus' birth, they say simply, clearly and repeatedly that *"The Holy Spirit will come upon you, and the power of the Most High will overshadow you. So the holy one to be born to you will be called the Son of God"* (Luke 1:35).

Option number three:
God's Son

Is it conceivable, believable that Jesus was born of a virgin? Several reasons cause this option to make the most sense:

• He was sinless.
If Jesus had been born to a man and woman, He would have been conceived in sin. Since He claimed to be without sin (John 8:46), it is critical to believe in the virgin birth so we don't contradict Jesus Himself.

• He was the Savior.
If Jesus was sinful, He could never have saved mankind from their sins. Only someone sinless could do that. That's why the angel announced, *". . . give him the name Jesus, because he will save the people from their sins"* (Matthew 1:21).

• He was a human/divine, physical phenomenon.
When we take a look at the scientific data, the virgin birth makes sense. We know that the female ovum contains half of the 46 chromosomes that are in every cell of the human body. The male sex cell adds the other 23. On contact, the two cells become one. The cell divides and then begins to grow,

building a complete body, mind and spirit. Reverently we can picture the Holy Spirit fashioning the necessary genes and chromosomes and then uniting with the body of the virgin with her 23 chromosomes. Then we can rightly describe Jesus as "one person" since He was conceived by the union of cells by which a single person is produced. And He has two natures—fully human and fully divine—since the cell which united with the human ovum was divine, and not human in origin.[8]

Fascinating!

Conclusion: He was not a child born but a Son given.

Most people read the story of Jesus' birth and think of a baby being born. Not so. Let's change our perspective. An estimated 60 billion people have lived on Planet Earth. But something happened in that manger that has never happened before or since. It was an event so powerful that we date our calendars by it. More happened than simply another child being born. God gave us His Son!

Matthew Henry summarized it well: "The God who took a motherless woman out of the side of a man, took a fatherless man out of the body of a woman."

Heavy Thoughts:

Looking Inside

Three options: illegitimate son, Joseph's son or God's son. One decision: Whose son was He? One promise: If this is a struggle intellectually or spiritually, remember that you can always go back and rely on the promises of God. For this decision, remember what the angel told Mary:

"For nothing is impossible with God" (Luke 1:37).

Dear Jesus:

Jesus with skin on:

"Hasta la vista, baby!" warned one of the great action heroes of all time—"Ahnold" Schwarzenegger. But Bruce Thomas, working with young people in Romania, tells a story that shows us who the Ultimate Action Hero really is.

"As the boys rushed me up to see their dormitory at the 'Casa de Copii' in Otelu-Rosu, I was almost out of breath. It was hard to believe that this was once a run-down bordello and bar that now housed around 70 orphaned children and staff. As we turned to go down the hall, Marius, who is eleven, insisted that I go into his room first. As we walked in, he and a herd of other boys, all clinging to my arms, slid the door closed behind them. As the door slid shut, it revealed a picture that I will never forget. The boys had been collecting these 'action hero' cards and had placed them in kind of a shrine on their wall. There were pictures of all of the great, muscle-bound action heroes of all times—Sylvester Stallone, Chuck Norris, Bruce Willis, Bruce Lee, Jean-Claude Van Damme and of course 'Ahnold' Schwarzenegger.

But it was evident that those guys were not the main attraction in this shrine of hulking heroes. Marius had placed an 8 x 10 picture of the ultimate action hero right in the middle of them. You guessed it. Right there in the place of honor, was a huge 'Bleeding Heart' picture of Jesus. He kind of looked out of place at first, but the more I thought about it, the more I realized that this setting was perfect for Him.

Jesus really is the greatest action hero of all times. Of course turning over a table or two wouldn't exactly qualify Him in today's market as the toughest good guy in town. But because He is the original 'good guy,' the newcomers have used a lot of His original material to make names for themselves. For example, Schwarzenegger's famous 'I'll be back' line is an obvious quote, taken out of context, from the Lord Himself. And all of the dynamic explosions on film haven't yet matched the walking on water incident or even come close to the raising from the dead scene yet.

But there were obviously a lot of differences between Jesus and this group of he-men too. Jesus was not a violent man and didn't blow anybody away. That was not His character or style. And though He didn't spend every waking moment at the gym, He did spend a lot of time building His Body!"

More Than Muscle Bound

Somehow people have seen Jesus as a wimp, as dull and boring, or as a narrow-minded fundamentalist with a long list of do's and don'ts. That's not Him at all. A true picture of Jesus reveals that He isn't a wimp, but the Ultimate Action Hero. During the three short years of His ministry, what made Him stand so far above all the other action heroes who have ever lived? We can put these pictures of Him on our wall:

Photo Number One: Come Some Day
Written over 700 years before Jesus was born, the book of Isaiah foretold the Messiah who would come some day. Look what this Messiah would do when He comes:

"The Spirit of the Sovereign Lord is on me, because the Lord has anointed me to preach good news to the poor. He has sent me to bind up the brokenhearted, to proclaim freedom for the captives and release from darkness for the prisoners, to proclaim the year of the Lord's favor and the day of vengeance of our God, to comfort all who mourn, and provide for those who grieve in Zion—to bestow

on them a crown of beauty instead of ashes, the oil of gladness instead of mourning, and a garment of praise instead of a spirit of despair. They will be called oaks of righteousness, a planting of the Lord for the display of his splendor" (Isaiah 61:1-3).

According to Isaiah, what was the Action Hero Messiah going to do?

- Preach good news to the poor.
- Bind up (heal) the brokenhearted.
- Proclaim freedom for the captives.

As He does these things, people who are grieving will be comforted. Those whose lives have turned to ashes will see beauty in their lives again. The ones who mourn will be happy again. Those who experience despair and depression will enter into enthusiastic praise.

Those who encounter the coming Messiah and the ministry He has to offer will become "oaks of righteousness." What's an "oak of righteousness"? An oak is a strong tree with deep roots. Righteousness means entering into a right relationship with the Messiah. That relationship leads to right thinking that results in right behavior. People whose roots go down deep in their relationship with the Messiah, will grow up strong and tall to show others how incredible He is.

Wow! That doesn't look too shabby! To a generation who has experienced tremendous grief, pain, depression and destruction of its hopes and dreams, the Messiah wants to turn all of that around and change us into "oaks of righteousness." Tack that photo on the wall!

Photo Number Two: Unroll the Scroll

Speed ahead 700 plus years to a large gathering in a small town. The hometown boy had returned. Invited to read the Scripture in the synagogue, He unrolled the scroll and read these words: *"The Spirit of the Lord is on me, because he has anointed me to preach good news to the poor. He has sent me to proclaim freedom for the prisoners and recovery of sight for the blind, to release the oppressed, to proclaim the year of the Lord's favor"* (Luke 4:18, 19).

Vaguely familiar? He read from Isaiah 61:1, 2. After He finished reading, He rolled up the scroll, gave it to the attendant and sat down. Everyone had their eyes fastened on Him. Then He told them: *"Today this scripture is fulfilled in your hearing"* (Luke 4:21).

Deathly silence. No one moved. No one spoke a word. You could hear a pin drop. Then those people got furious. They drove Him out of town, took Him to the brow of a hill so they could throw Him off the cliff.

Jesus proclaimed Himself the Messiah. They did not like it one bit. But that didn't matter. The question is: Did He do the things that the Messiah talked about? Did He preach good news to the poor, bind up (heal) the brokenhearted and proclaim freedom for the captives? Did He do that? All we have to do is thumb through the pages of Matthew, Mark, Luke and John to see that on page after page we see Jesus preaching the good news, healing the sick and delivering the oppressed.

When John the Baptist (another great action hero) heard about this from his prison cell, he sent someone to ask Jesus about it. Jesus told them to go back and tell John what they saw and heard: *"The blind receive sight, the lame walk, those who have leprosy are cured, the deaf hear, the dead are raised, and the good news is preached to the poor"* (Matthew 11:4, 5).

At another point Matthew wrote: *"Jesus went throughout Galilee, teaching in their synagogues, preaching the good news of the kingdom, and healing every disease and sickness among the people. News about him spread all over Syria, and people brought to him all who were ill with various diseases, those suffering severe pain, the demon-possessed, those having seizures, and the paralyzed, and he healed them"* (Matthew 4:23, 24).

Later, Matthew gave a similar description, but this time he shows us what drove Jesus to do what He did. Can you find it? *"Jesus went through all the towns and villages, teaching in their synagogues, preaching the good news of the kingdom and healing every disease and sickness. When he saw the crowds, he had compassion on them, because they were harassed and helpless, like sheep without a shepherd"* (Matthew 9:35, 36).

This only scratches the surface of Jesus' ministry of preaching, healing and delivering—all in only one of the four Gospels! Hundreds of parables, stories, healings and miracles cover the pages of the Gospels. For example, we know that Jesus healed at least nine different blind people, many who had been blind from birth. At the end of the Gospel of John we get an idea of how much Jesus did beyond what was written down. *"Jesus did many other things as well. If every one of them were written down, I suppose that even the whole world would not have room for the books that would be written"* (John 21:25).

One action hero said: "You gotta say what you mean and mean what you say!" If that's true, then Jesus was the greatest preacher, teacher, miracle-worker and healer of all time! He said what He meant and meant what He said. Put a pin in that picture and stick it to the wall!

Photo Number Three: Make a Copy

It's one thing for Jesus to do all of this amazing stuff; after all, He is the Messiah. But He taught His disciples to do it too! What they did is like a photocopy of what Jesus did. The Ultimate Action Hero multiplied Himself.

Jesus showed them how to preach good news to the poor, bind up the brokenhearted and proclaim freedom for the captives.

Then He set up a mission trip for them. He called them together for a little orientation. Among other things, Jesus told them, *"As you go, preach this message: 'The kingdom of heaven is near.' Heal the sick, raise the dead, cleanse those who have leprosy, drive out demons. Freely you have received, freely give"* (Matthew 10:7, 8).

Then Jesus sent them out two by two. What did they do? *"They went out and preached that people should repent. They drove out many demons and anointed many sick people with oil and healed them"* (Mark 6:12, 13).

Like a CD that gets stuck and plays the same song over and over, the same topics keep coming up again and again—preaching, healing and delivering. But now instead of Jesus doing it all, He gave His disciples the authority to do it. That meant the ministry of Jesus could spread beyond one person to many. At this point, the pictures to tack on the wall start to multiply!

Photo Number Four: Spread the Fun

Now we get to the exciting part. Fasten your seat belt. Grab your hat. Put on your sunglasses. Roll up your bulletproof windows. You're about to get blown away. Jesus did almost all of His ministry by:
- Preaching the good news
- Healing the sick
- Delivering the demon-possessed

Then Jesus taught His disciples to minister to people by doing the same. Are you on the edge of your seat? Get ready! Jesus wants you and me to help the people around us by:
- Preaching the good news
- Healing the sick
- Delivering the demon-possessed

"C'mon. You're kidding me! I could never do that!" we say. Not so fast. Jesus told us we could and we should. *"I tell you the truth, anyone who has faith in me will do what I have been doing. He will do even greater things than these, because I am going to the Father"* (John 14:12).

Who is "anyone"? I did an in-depth study of this in Greek and I discovered that "anyone" means "anyone"! So "anyone" includes not only pastors and missionaries, not just adults, but you and me. It includes anyone who believes in Jesus and seeks to do His will. He tells us to ask for anything in His name and He will do it (John 14:13, 14).

Then He put the icing on the cake: *"He will do even greater things than these, because I am going to the Father."* Greater than Jesus? Give me a break! No. These works are not greater in quality. How could we ever do anything with more quality than Jesus? But we (all of us together) will do them in much greater quantity. That means that all of us get in on the action. Following Jesus is not a spectator sport. It all started (not ended) when Jesus ascended to the Father and released His Holy Spirit to live inside of us. The greater things we would do would be accomplished because of the strength of the Holy Spirit. Now we have His power and His authority to do the same ministry that Jesus did.

Does it work? You bet! Just look at these real examples:

• Preaching

Steve, a ninth grader, let Jesus take control of his life over the Christmas break. He made a commitment to go back to his school and stand strong for Jesus. He made a "Ten Most Wanted List"—writing down the names of students for whom he wanted to pray and witness. Within two months nine of the ten had decided to follow Christ. The tenth one received Christ two years later. Within two months over 60 students were meeting for a junior high Bible study. They shared the good news of Jesus with every student in their school!

• Healing

Last school year my daughter Katie's good friend Pat got pneumonia. He went from a cough to an aggravated cough to pneumonia to intensive care in the hospital where he hovered between life and death for weeks. The battle was on for his life. Students prayed by the hundreds, some at the hospital and some at school. They prayed for weeks on end. Finally, the breakthrough came and he has had a remarkable recovery. He was supposed to be in rehab for two months. Remarkably, he was finished in only four days! God, not the teens, performed the healing, but He responded mightily to the intercession of so many students.

• Delivering

A student I know in Charlotte, North Carolina, had become so depressed that he decided to commit suicide one night. Some high school friends of this student live in Atlanta. They heard that he was depressed, so they met together to pray for him. Only later did they learn that the very hour they prayed was the hour when he was close to killing himself. But during that hour he made a radical turn and did not commit suicide. We need to be careful not to assume that all depression is brought on by demon possession. Often there are physical factors as well. But, in some cases, it is brought on by the power of Satan and it calls for persistent prayer on the part of God's people for deliverance.

This list of action examples could become lengthy. Students, not satisfied with the status quo, call on God, take action to experience the ministry of Jesus, and see the power of God demonstrated before their very eyes. And you can too! When you jump into the action, you will have to reserve a whole wall to hold all the Ultimate Action Hero pictures. And you will be in each one—with the Hero Himself!

Body Building

My friend Bruce finished his story like this:

"I read something Arnold Schwarzenegger wrote that challenged me to 'build myself up' for this battle. He said:

'In Austria when I was 15 years old and was just getting started in body building, the only way I could learn was to listen and copy the more advanced bodybuilders training in the gym. Looking back I can see how little any of us knew at the time. All we had to go on were some basic principles that had been passed on from one to another and written about in magazines. We studied these magazines with such intensity it nearly burned the print right off the pages. I had to learn about training, diet, nutrition . . . and all the other elements of training by trial and error. It took a lot of effort and a very long time. However, my ambition to become a great bodybuilder has been the driving force in my life, and so I learned what I had to do, whatever the cost.'

I think Arnold's plan is similar to Jesus' desire for us. Jesus wants to be 'the driving force in my life,' and yours too! He has designed us to 'preach, heal and deliver' just like He did. To get in on that we must learn how to do it—whatever the cost!"

Now it's time to swing into action. Hasta la vista, baby!

Up Close and Personal

1. *Who is your favorite action hero? After reading this chapter, why do you think Jesus is the greatest Hero?*

2. *Recall at least three (or more) incidents in the books of Matthew, Mark, Luke and John of Jesus preaching, healing and delivering.*

3. *Why do you think Jesus passed on His ministry to His disciples and then to us?*

4. *Do you think "anyone" in John 14:12 includes you? Specifically what do you need to do about that?*

5. *Give one concrete, personal example in which you have seen the ministry of Jesus at work.*

6. *Think about one way you want Jesus to be more of an "action hero" to you.*

The Life and Ministry of Jesus

Imperfect Parents day **1**

*"If Christ came back today, would he be an alternative rocker? In his day he was something of a
counterculturist, hanging out with lepers, driving Pharisees and Roman governors to distraction, suffering little children to come to him no matter what the stuffy old adults thought. So, were he around
today, would he be ministering to disaffected youth?"*[1]
—Time *magazine*

Checking It Out

Report cards are the pits! Come home with B's and C's and your parents say, "C is average. Make all
B's." So you hustle. The next report card: all B's. Yeah! Your parents say, "That shows you can study;
make some A's." You study and get some A's. Your parents say, "I knew you could. If you can get a couple of A's, you can get *all* A's." Going all out, you get all A's. You're excited. Your parents should be too.
But they say, "That's nice. But when I was in school we walked five miles to school . . . one way . . .
barefoot . . . uphill . . . in the snow." Yeah, right! Parents are a trip!

Jesus, the Son of God, lived with imperfect parents like you do. How did He handle His relationship
with them?

When He was a teenager, Jesus got separated from His parents. They panicked.

His parents did not know what to think. *"'Son!' his mother said to him. 'Why have you done this to us?
Your father and I have been frantic, searching for you everywhere.' 'But why did you need to search?' he
asked."*

**"'You should have known that I would be in my Father's house.' But they
didn't understand what he meant" (Luke 2:48, 49, NLT).**

Hot Notes:

Getting the Point

Read the whole account in Luke 2:41-52.

Nobody has a perfect home. Some homes are less perfect than others. Whatever our home situation, we
have hassles. Some deal with minor issues like driving the car, curfew and dating. Others struggle with deeper issues like parents fighting, divorce, abuse—verbal, physical and sexual. Home can be a tough place
sometimes. Jesus lived with flawed parents, Mary and Joseph. In the only recorded incident from His
teenage years, we learn a lot about Him by the way He dealt with His parents. And we can learn how to handle our relationships with our parents too. Look at some of the problems Jesus had with His parents:

• His parents dragged Him along.

"Every year Jesus' parents went to Jerusalem for the Passover festival. When Jesus was twelve years old, they attended the festival as usual" (Luke 2:41, 42, NLT).

Jesus' parents insisted that He go on this religious trip. Could Jesus have thought, "Boooorrrrriiinnng!"? We don't know. But we do know that today many people avoid God because their parents crammed religion down their throats.

• His parents had a communication breakdown.

The family had traveled a long distance to Jerusalem. And it was a long way home.

"After the celebration was over, they started home to Nazareth, but Jesus stayed behind in Jerusalem. His parents didn't miss him at first, because they assumed he was with friends among the other travelers. But when he didn't show up that evening, they started to look for him among their relatives and friends" (Luke 2:43, 44, NLT)

Jesus' parents started home. Jesus didn't. They thought He was with friends. He wasn't. Somebody dropped the ball somewhere. That miscommunication between parents and teen can happen a million different ways.

• His parents panicked.

Nothing produces tension like a panicked parent.

"When they couldn't find him, they went back to Jerusalem to search for him there. Three days later they finally discovered him" (Luke 2:45, 46, NLT).

When parents panic, they tend to put the clamps on and overreact. We can help the situation by not panicking ourselves and overreacting to their overreaction!

• His parents felt mistreated.

Parents like respect. They appreciate appreciation. In this case Mary and Joseph didn't feel respected or appreciated.

"His parents didn't know what to think. 'Son!' his mother said to him. 'Why have you done this to us? Your father and I have been frantic, searching for you everywhere'" (Luke 2:48, NLT).

We can hear the hurt in Mary's voice. Unresolved hurt leads from anger to bitterness to hate. Many problems with our parents exist because of unresolved past hurts. Either we hurt them or they hurt us.

• His parents didn't understand Him.

"My parents just don't understand me!" Ever said that? This week? Sometimes we operate on different wavelengths from our parents. That can cause problems. That happened with Jesus and His parents.

"'But why did you need to search?' he asked. 'You should have known that I would be in my Father's house.' But they didn't understand what he meant" (Luke 2:49, 50, NLT).

Jesus' parents didn't understand. Sometimes yours don't either. But that doesn't mean we get mad at them or cut off the relationship. The challenge? To understand them. Which of these five problems do you struggle with most? What can you do about it?

Parent Problem-Solving

God gave us our parents for a reason. Think about it—we are unique because we were born to and raised by our particular parents. God wants to use our parents—good or bad—to mold and shape our lives into what He wants them to be. Understanding that, we must make a decision, like Jesus did, to respond correctly to our problems with our parents.

If we respond incorrectly, we will have problems with our parents and with our Heavenly Father. If we respond positively, like Jesus, we can create a better relationship with our parents and God. How did

Jesus handle these problems with His parents?

• He saw the issue from His parents' perspective.

Jesus made a decision to go along with His parents even though possibly He didn't want to. Instead of pulling against His parents, He decided to cooperate with them.

Question: *Will you stop rebelling against your parents because they have not done things to suit you?*

• He started with pure motives.

The communication breakdown Jesus had with His parents didn't come from rebellion—trying to get His own way, but from His desire to do His Father's will.

"Three days later they finally discovered him. He was in the Temple, sitting among the religious teachers, discussing deep questions with them" (Luke 2:46, NLT).

Question: *Have your motives been to please God or to get your own way?*

• He had settled the self-esteem issue.

Jesus' parents didn't understand Him, but He was willing to live with that because He knew who He was and what God had called Him to do.

He asked, *"Didn't you know I had to be in my Father's house?"* (Luke 2:49).

Just as Jesus knew who He was, we, too, can know who we are in Christ. Without being super-spiritual or judgmental, we can live positively even with parents who don't agree.

Question: *Are you willing to be misunderstood by your parents if you are headed in a different spiritual direction from them?*

• He submitted to His parents.

Jesus' parents did not understand, and He did not agree with them, but He submitted to them. *"Then he returned to Nazareth with them and was obedient to them. . . ."* (Luke 2:51, NLT).

And, boy, was His mom proud of Him!

". . . But his mother treasured all these things in her heart" (Luke 2:51).

His mom knew who He was, yet when He submitted to His parents, it confirmed everything she knew. Is it possible that our parents don't respect us more because we don't obey them?

Question: *Is what you say about Jesus backed up by obeying your parents?*

Positive Results

Jesus' positive response to His parents, even with their problems swirling around led to Him becoming a balanced, healthy person who could respond to His Heavenly Father correctly. When, like Jesus, we choose to respond correctly to our parents, then we have freedom—freedom to love our parents and our Heavenly Father and to develop to our fullest potential.

"So Jesus grew both in height and in wisdom, and he was loved by God and by all who knew him" (Luke 2:52, NLT).

Jesus lived a balanced life physically, mentally, spiritually and socially.

- Jesus grew in "height." He kept His body in excellent physical condition.
- Jesus stretched His mind in the pursuit of knowledge and viewed that knowledge from God's perspective. That's wisdom—looking at life from God's viewpoint.
- Jesus knew His Father loved and accepted Him. And He loved His Father. That formed the basis of their relationship.
- All who knew Him loved Him. He interacted with and enjoyed people no matter what their social standing—even adults. He showed genuine love for them.

What an example for us! We can live like Jesus too, because His Spirit empowers us. With a proper response to imperfect parents, we learn healthy balance in our homes.

Heavy Thoughts:

Looking Inside

Looking at Jesus' relationship with His parents, it's obvious that to have a healthy, balanced life we must respond properly to our parents.
   Ask yourself these questions:
   In what ways are my parents imperfect?

   How do I need to respond to them?

   What positive results will I experience when I respond to my parents the way Jesus did?

Dear Jesus:

Jesus with skin on:

"Jesus' baptism resembles raising a flag on a ship. The flag identifies what country the ship belongs to. Here Jesus publicly raised His flag to make it clear that He had come as the Messiah."
—Barry St. Clair

Checking It Out

The water was freezing! I stood in it up to my waist—waiting. The man next to me talked to the people on the riverbank—about eighty of them. But I didn't understand a word he said. I was standing in a river in the mountains of Romania. We had not gathered for a swimming party, but for a baptism. The man beside me told the crowd what that meant in Romanian. One by one, ten of them came into the water and I dunked them under it. But before I did, each one spoke to the crowd telling them that they had embraced Christ and wanted to be baptized; they wanted everyone to know they were followers of Jesus. When they came out of the water, there were hugs all around, and not a dry eye on the riverbank. When Romania was under Communist rule, if a person chose to be baptized, it could cost him his job, educational opportunities and in some cases life itself. It's serious business!

"One day Jesus came from Nazareth in Galilee, and he was baptized by John in the Jordan River. And when Jesus came up out of the water, he saw the heavens split open and the Holy Spirit descending like a dove on him. And a voice came from heaven saying, 'You are my beloved Son, and I am fully pleased with you'" (Mark 1:9-11, NLT).

Hot Notes:

_____

_____

_____

_____

_____

Getting the Point

Jesus' baptism ranks right up there with the top events of His life. Each of the four Gospel writers described it. For Jesus, baptism was an act of obedience to His Heavenly Father. In the same way Jesus considered it important, we, too, need to see its significance for our lives.

Presented to the Public

When Jesus was baptized by John the Baptist, Jesus' purpose was to present Himself for public ministry. John, the voice crying in the wilderness (Mark 1:3), knew his job was to make that announcement.

"He announced: 'Someone is coming soon who is far greater than I am—so much greater that I am not even worthy to be his slave. I baptize you with water, but he will baptize you with the Holy Spirit!'" (Mark 1:7, 8, NLT).

Here Jesus publicly made it clear that He had come as the Messiah.

Power for Ministry

John baptized Jesus in the Jordan River. John put Jesus in the water and then He came up out of the water. When that happened, Jesus saw the heavens open up and the Holy Spirit descending like a dove on Him.

If you have seen a movie about Jesus' life, the baptism scene always depicts the Holy Spirit in the form of a dove, coming down and landing on Jesus' shoulder. Actually, in the original language the Holy Spirit descended *into* Him. Jesus was born by the Holy Spirit—the Holy Spirit was His Father instead of Joseph. But at His baptism, the Holy Spirit empowered Him in a special way that equipped Him for His ministry as the Messiah. This dynamic event launched Jesus into the public ministry He came to do. It gave Him the power and authority to carry out His unique role.

Pleasing the Father

At the same time the Holy Spirit came into Him, this incident took another unique twist. A voice came from Heaven, saying, *"You are my Son, whom I love; with you I am well pleased"* (Mark 1:11).

A voice came from Heaven only three times in the New Testament: at Jesus' baptism, at His transfiguration and at the cross. Each experience affirmed Jesus' purpose in coming and showed that another dimension beyond the physical realm was in effect—the spiritual dimension.

When God spoke to Jesus, we can hear Him make four incredible statements about the relationship between the Father and the Son:

1. The word translated "You" is a word used only for Deity. The Father used it to show Jesus as distinct and unique from all others.
2. "Whom I love" expresses that Jesus is the special object of His Father's affection. He is special and chosen.
3. "Son" tells us that God was Jesus' own, unique, personal Father. Jesus had special access to His Father.
4. "I am well pleased" means that God took special pleasure in Jesus from the beginning of time. Jesus never did anything to displease His Father. Knowing how hard it is for us to obey our parents, we can see how awesome that is. Jesus' obedience created the unique relationship. Without it, Jesus would have lost His unique right to be God's Son. Jesus obeyed at baptism. That's why the Father came down to affirm Him. He carried that same obedience through to the cross.

Plunging into Baptism

Jesus was baptized as a 30-year-old man just ready to begin His public ministry. At the end of His physical life on earth He gave a command—a commission—to all of His future followers. He said, *"All authority in heaven and on earth has been given to me. Therefore go and make disciples of all nations,* [people groups] *baptizing them in the name of the Father and of the Son and of the Holy Spirit, and teaching them to obey everything I have commanded you. And surely I am with you always, to the very end of the age"* (Matthew 28:18-20).

These words do not present an option, but a command. Once a person decides to follow Jesus, he or she needs to obey Christ by getting baptized.

The word "baptize" actually means "to dip." Picture a large container full of dye. Dipping the garment in the dye to change its color expresses the idea of "baptize." By going into the water, we identify with Jesus. Going into the water means that just as Jesus died, was buried and then raised from the dead, we too die to our sinful nature, are buried and are raised up to new life.

All through the New Testament the only people who were baptized were believers. That carried through to the end of the fifth century. If someone gets baptized before becoming a believer, that person only gets wet. If someone gets baptized after becoming a believer, that person experiences real baptism. You may want to do further study on baptism yourself and discuss this with the spiritual leaders at your church. But, be sure you follow the Lord's example by being baptized in water as a follower of Jesus Christ.

Heavy Thoughts:

Looking Inside

Following Jesus' example in baptism, we need to be baptized as an act of obedience to Christ—in order to raise our flag for Jesus, letting the whole world know that we follow Him!

"We were therefore buried with him through baptism into death in order that, just as Christ was raised from the dead through the glory of the Father, we too may live a new life" (Romans 6:4).

Dear Jesus:

Jesus with skin on:

Roadkill Grill

*"In short, Satan was offering Jesus the chance to be the thundering Messiah we think we want. . . .
We want anything but a Suffering Messiah."*[2]
—Philip Yancey

Checking It Out

The Roadkill Grill boasts, "You kill it. We grill it." Some of their entrees include: The Chicken (that didn't cross the road), Flat Cat (served in a single or in a stack), Road Toad à la Mode and Poodles 'N Noodles.

We become like those menu items when we give in to temptation. Satan tempted Jesus to try to make Him spiritual roadkill too.

"Jesus . . . was led by the Spirit in the desert, where for forty days he was tempted by the devil. He ate nothing during those days, and at the end of them he was hungry" (Luke 4:1, 2).

Hot Notes:

Getting the Point

Read Luke 4:1-13.

The scene: The wilderness in Judea, called "the Devastation," extended 35 miles by 15 miles. Hills looked like dust heaps, bare rocks had jagged edges, the limestone blistered and peeled, the ground sounded hollow. During the day the ground glowed like a huge furnace. The cliffs rose 1200 feet, then swooped down to the Dead Sea.

Here Satan appeared to Jesus to get Him to compromise His character. Instead Jesus used it to *build* His character. Similarly, Satan tempts us to make us spiritual roadkill. Our response either destroys us or makes us stronger.

Appealing to Physical Appetites

Satan came to Jesus after He had fasted forty days. Can you imagine! Jesus was *really* hungry. Then the devil said to him, *"Since you're God's Son, command this stone to turn into a loaf of bread"* (Luke 4:3, The Message).

Covered with limestone chunks, the wilderness looked like mega-loaves of bread. Satan tempted Jesus to satisfy physical appetites incorrectly. Satan tries to make us spiritual roadkill by tempting us to use our physical appetites incorrectly as well.

Food—we need it to live. But Satan has so messed us up that most people are either "junk-food junkies" or struggling with eating disorders. Example: soft drinks addict us to sugar since they have twelve teaspoons in each one. So we switch to diet drinks, which are 300 times sweeter than regular drinks! Satan takes something good and makes it harmful.

Sex—is fantastic—inside of marriage. But Satan wants us to "do it" his way, not God's way, because he knows it will destroy us. Two teenagers are attracted to each other. One thing leads to another. Holding hands turns into super-holding hands. (The girl strokes the guy's arm with her fingers. He looks cool on the outside, but is yelling "Yeeeooooowww" on the inside.) Kissing moves on to super-kissing (the roto-rooter types!) and hugging to super-hugging (It's a wrestling match in the back seat!). And, before you know it, you are doing things that should be saved for marriage.

Jesus replied to Satan with an answer that suggested He had thought about it before. He told him, *"No! The Scriptures say, 'People need more than bread for their life'"* (Luke 4:4, NLT).

Jesus stared temptation down by going straight to the Bible: *". . . man does not live on bread alone but on every word that comes from the mouth of the LORD"* (Deuteronomy 8:3).

In Satan's face, Jesus made two points clear:
- A person does not get satisfaction from "feeding your face" with physical desires.
- To whip Satan, we need to know the Bible.

"How can a young man [or woman] keep his way pure? By living according to your word. . . . I have hidden your word in my heart that I might not sin against you" (Psalm 119:9, 11).

Decide to know the Bible like Jesus did by memorizing one verse a week.

Longing for Material Things

They stood on a mountain looking out as far as the eye could see. Satan pointed out all the kingdoms of the earth to Jesus. The devil said, *"They're yours in all their splendor to serve your pleasure. I'm in charge of them all and can turn them over to whomever I wish. Worship me and they're yours, the whole works"* (Luke 4:6, 7, The Message).

Satan tried to destroy Jesus' ministry by promising what he thought Jesus wanted. How stupid! Jesus already had everything He wanted and the power to enjoy it.

Satan lures us by promising us "stuff." "Have whatever you want—new clothes, stereo, CDs, new car." His desire is that we love things and use people. God desires that we love people and use things!

When we give in to our desires for material things, we become consumed with loving "stuff." We feed our selfishness. Satan knows that will destroy us. (Why does the most affluent nation on the face of the planet have the highest rate of divorce, abuse and suicide?) Pursuing material things is like drinking seawater: the more you drink, the more you want.

Gradually, Satan gets our eyes off the goal. We become "casual Christians," reducing God to fit into our materialistic box. At that point we become spiritual roadkill.

Jesus says, *"No one can serve two masters. Either he will hate the one and love the other, or he will be devoted to the one and despise the other. You cannot serve both God and Money"* (Matthew 6:24).

We overcome our desire for material things the same way Jesus did. He replied, *"It is written: 'Worship the Lord your God and serve him only'"* (Luke 4:8). Again Jesus stared this temptation in the eyes by quoting the Bible.

Set a goal to worship God every day, using the Psalms to do so.

Desiring Thrills and Chills

Satan appealed to Jesus' imagination by taking Him on a fantasy trip. The devil took Him to Jerusalem, to the highest point of the temple, and said, *"If you are God's Son, jump. It's written, isn't it, that 'he has placed you in the care of angels to protect you; they will catch you; so you won't so much as stub your toe on a stone'?"* (Luke 4:9-11, The Message).

Satan made one last, desperate effort to destroy Jesus by trying to get Him to do something sensational to gain popularity. The drop from the pinnacle of the temple is 450 feet to the Kidron Valley below. If Jesus had done what Satan asked, He would have landed on the ground without being hurt. And the people would have made Him king.

If Jesus had fallen for it, it would not have increased His popularity. Instead it would have destroyed Him—spiritual roadkill. In the same way, Satan wants to destroy us by tempting us with false popularity and cheap thrills. Popularity rarely lasts. Why do people start smoking, drinking and doing drugs? They want attention. When they get caught with drugs, where are their friends then? Satan wants us to give our time and energy to things that don't last.

In his final, desperate temptation, Satan quoted the Bible to Jesus (Psalm 91:11, 12), like Jesus had been quoting it to him. Jesus saw the trick. He responded with the Scripture, *"Do not test the LORD your God"* (Deuteronomy 6:16).

Jesus' challenge to beat Satan when he entices us with popularity and thrills: resist the pressure to do "stupid stuff" to impress others and decide to obey God instead.

Heavy Thoughts:

ⓛooking Inside

To avoid the Roadkill Grill, we must take action to stand against these powerful temptations.
- *Overcome physical appetites by memorizing Scripture. Start with 1 Corinthians 10:13; Hebrews 2:18; 4:15.*
- *Overcome the longing for material things by taking the focus off of "stuff" and focus on daily worshiping God. Read a Psalm every day.*
- *Overcome the desire for popularity and thrills by not trying to impress people but trying to please Jesus by obeying Him. Take one action to obey God every day.*

Dear Jesus:

Jesus with skin on:

"The illustrated teachings of Christ fall into three categories. First there are the eighteen major stories for which Jesus' teachings are most remembered. There are sixty-seven analogies where Jesus does quick comparisons of his truths to ordinary, understandable images. And finally . . . there are sixteen metaphors in the gospel of John, where Jesus refers to himself as bread, light, water or the Good Shepherd."[3]
—*Calvin Miller*

We could fill several books with the teaching and preaching of Jesus. Here we will look at one brief teaching representing all the rest and see how radical He really is!

Checking It Out

Like "The Fonz" on the TV show "Happy Days," Doug Farmer had slicked-back hair, black boots, black leather jacket and loooooonnng fingernails. And he picked on me in the seventh grade. That's the grade both of us were in, although I suspect he should have been in tenth grade. One day in PE he scratched me with those long nails. That was it! I threw him to the floor. As we beat the stew out of each other, Coach Chick Dalton walked in. He stopped the fight, put boxing gloves on us, and we went at it again. We beat each other silly. I wanted to kill him!

That's the way I sometimes want to handle it when I have a problem with someone. But Jesus' approach was radically different.

"But if you are willing to listen, I say, love your enemies. Do good to those who hate you. Pray for the happiness of those who curse you. Pray for those who hurt you. If someone slaps you on one cheek, turn the other cheek. If someone demands your coat, offer your shirt also. Give what you have to anyone who asks you for it; and when things are taken away from you, don't try to get them back. Do for others as you would like them to do for you" (Luke 6:27-31, NLT).

Hot Notes:

Getting the Point

Read the whole account in Luke 6:27-36.

In the middle of Luke's version of the Sermon on the Mount, the most radical sermon ever preached, Jesus challenged every natural instinct we have. He knew some people were not going to hear it. That's why He said, *"But if you are willing to listen. . . ."* If we approach Jesus' teachings with our minds made up, we'll miss it every time. But if we hear it with open ears, then we will have open hearts to respond radically with an open hand to others.

Jesus gets to the bottom line very quickly: *"Love your enemies."* Who is He talking about? Those we hate (such as Doug Farmer). We can't hate someone we don't know. So our enemies are not "out there" but "in here"—those close enough to have done something to us. Not the IRS, our school system, or a terrorist group; but family, church, friends and former friends. An enemy is any relationship where we have drawn a battle line.

Radical Choices
• We are called to love them.
Love is an attitude. Jesus used a word for love that does not indicate the passionate love of a man for a woman, or the affectionate love of a close friend—but a love that is beyond earthly love. Unlike all other kinds of love, this love comes from God. It is a love that is deeply devoted. Jesus demonstrated it on the cross. We can't create it because God is its source. When Jesus lives in us, we have the potential to love our enemies. We love "in spite of" what another person has done to us.

With God's love in us, we can desire their highest good for an enemy. Instead of wishing them the worst, we can wish them the best. The other person may never change. This kind of love doesn't wait until they do. We love them now. Love is a choice—and it's the best choice.

• We are called to do good to them.
In Jesus' day the Jews lived under Roman rule. They hated the Romans like cats hate dogs. The only reaction to the Romans was retaliation. To retaliate means, "You did it to me, so now I am going to do it to you—but even harder." Rather, Jesus compels us to speak positive words and take positive actions.

First, Jesus says to pray for the happiness of those who curse you (Luke 6:28). When someone says something bad about us, Jesus says to talk to God about them. That gives us God's perspective.

Next, He says to pray for those who hurt you. When someone does something to physically harm us, which is even more difficult than verbal abuse, we are still to bring the situation to God in prayer.

As we talk to God about the situation, He wants us to be honest with Him. There may be a time when you need to say, "Jesus, this person hates my guts. Honestly, I hate his [or her] guts. I'm angry. But I am bringing it to You. Calm my feelings and help me do what You would do."

It may take many times of coming to God with this, even several times a day, to get our hearts in tune with His. But prayer is the only beginning point for loving our enemies.

In addition to positive words, Jesus expects us to take positive actions—radical actions. He says, *"If someone strikes you on one cheek, turn to him the other also"* (Luke 6:29).

"Cheek" includes the jaw. This is not a light slap to the face, but a hard punch to the side of the face. Jesus says: "Now that he has punched your lights out on one side, let him punch your lights out on the other." In essence we say, "Hit me again if it will make you feel better."

Then Jesus says, *"If someone demands your coat, offer your shirt also"* (Luke 6:29, NLT). Jesus doesn't want us to hold back anything. The "coat" was the outer garment; the "shirt" the undergarment. Jesus is saying, "If he wants your underwear, give it to him."

Doing good to our enemies is definitely a radical choice.

• We are called to give to them.
Where your enemy is concerned, *"Give what you have to anyone who asks you for it; and when things are taken away from you, don't try to get them back"* (Luke 6:30, NLT). Jesus is not saying, "Be careless with your money." It's deeper than that. When we have Jesus' point of view, we can choose to deprive ourselves of everything if necessary in order to restore the relationship. Even though this makes no human sense, God will honor our choices and bless us beyond our ability to comprehend.

Jesus challenges us to go beyond the love sinners have for each other (Luke 6:32-34). Ordinary love means that you love those who love you. But, extraordinary love means that you love those who hate you. An ordinary action is to repay good deeds for good deeds. But, an extraordinary action is to repay good deeds for bad deeds. Ordinary giving means lending only if the money comes back with interest. But, extraordinary giving means lending with no strings attached.

Jesus draws three significant conclusions that help us respond His way to our enemies:

- **The Golden Rule**
  Many cultures and religions have a golden rule, but they are always negatively expressed. For example: "What you hate, do not do to anyone else." Only Jesus expressed it positively, *"Do to others as you would have them do to you"* (Luke 6:31). The point is that we actively do good things for others. The Golden Rule covers all of life's relationships.

- **The Great Reward**
  When we respond to our enemies Jesus' way, then our reward will be great (Luke 6:35).

- **The Genuine Reproduction**
  Like Father, like children! We love like He loves. That reflects His compassionate character. You must be merciful just as your Father is merciful (Luke 6:36). That's radical Christianity!

Heavy Thoughts:

Looking Inside

Through Jesus, we have the resources to love, do good and give to our enemies.
Who is your enemy?
What radical actions of Jesus do you need to express to that person?
In what specific ways will you do it?

Dear Jesus:

Jesus with skin on:

The Touch

"A miracle is an event beyond the power of any known physical law to produce; it is a spiritual occurrence produced by the power of God, a marvel, a wonder. . . . Clearly, the wonders performed by Jesus Christ and the apostles authenticated their claim of authority and gave certitude to their message. . . . And at strategic moments God again and again manifested Himself to men by miracles so they had outward, confirming evidence that the words they heard from God's servants were true."[4]
—Billy Graham

Of the hundreds of healing miracles Jesus did, we will take a close look at one.

Checking It Out

Our two-year-old son, Scott, had been sick. That evening his temperature soared to 104 degrees and continued climbing. His body went limp and convulsions began. I panicked, running through the house yelling. I ran out in the yard—still yelling! Nobody was even there to yell at. I ran to the neighbors house—yelling! In my panic, I forgot to call 911. My only thought: "He's dying!" Out of control, I had this horrible, sick feeling inside. Desperately I prayed, "Lord, don't let my little boy die!"

The paramedics came and saved his life. But I have never forgotten that desperate feeling. It must have been the same feeling that rushed over a man named Jairus.

"On the other side of the lake the crowds received Jesus with open arms because they had been waiting for him. And now a man named Jairus, a leader of the local synagogue, came and fell down at Jesus' feet, begging him to come home with him. His only child was dying, a little girl twelve years old" (Luke 8:40-42, NLT).

Hot Notes:

- -
- -
- -
- -

Getting the Point

To get the whole story, read Luke 8:40-56.
Jesus' hand touched desperate people and healed them. How did that happen?

An Atmosphere of Openness

Jesus could meet these people's needs because they wanted Him to. *". . . the crowds received Jesus with open arms because they had been waiting for him"* (Luke 8:40, NLT).

Contrast this crowd with another crowd. *"And because of their unbelief, he couldn't do any mighty miracles among them except to place his hands on a few sick people and heal them. And he was amazed at their unbelief"* (Mark 6:5, 6, NLT).

It's pretty easy to become skeptical. We may say things like, "When I prayed before, nothing happened," "This problem is too big even for God" or "I don't think Jesus still does that today."

Fear, doubt and preconceived ideas that box God in can cause unbelief. However, if we welcome Jesus into every situation and eagerly expect Him to do something, like these people did, amazing things will take place.

I prayed for a young man with chronic mononucleosis. His parents had done everything. They asked me to pray for him. I did. Jesus healed him! Neither Jesus, nor I, make any promises that if you pray someone will be healed. But if we don't pray, then we close off the opportunity for God to work. If we do pray, many more people will experience Jesus' miraculous touch!

An Attitude of Faith

Both Jairus and the bleeding woman had an attitude of faith. How did they express it? As a *"leader of the local synagogue,"* Jairus had a good reputation in the community. He wasn't some wacko.

- He took an action step of faith by coming to Jesus.
- He *"fell at Jesus' feet."* As synagogue leader with a good education, prestige and money, pride could have kept him away. But he swallowed his pride and came to Jesus in humility. Humility is seeing how small we are and how big God is. It is the basis of faith.
- He was *"begging him."* His twelve-year-old daughter, the light of his life, lay dying. Jairus was a desperate man. Desperation encourages faith.

As Jesus headed toward Jairus' house, the crowd moved with Him to see what He would do. Walking the narrow streets, the crowd clamored to get close to Jesus, crushing against Him.

"And a woman was there who had been subject to bleeding for twelve years, but no one could heal her. She came up behind him and touched the edge of his cloak, and immediately her bleeding stopped" (Luke 8:43, 44).

- The woman with the hemorrhage had distressing physical consequences of her illness, but even worse social consequences, cutting her off from friends and from life. The spiritual consequences posed the biggest problems. According to Jewish law, the bleeding made her "ceremonially unclean." That meant she could not worship at the temple. She had financial consequences as well, having spent everything she had on doctors. This woman came to Jesus in desperation.
- She *"came up behind"* Jesus. Because of embarrassment she wanted to stay in the crowd, trying not to be noticed. But like a magnet, she was drawn to Jesus. With huge courage she got close enough to reach out and touch His robe. She took a faith action step.
- She touched the fringe of His robe, the end of a square cloth thrown over the left shoulder, hung down the back to the ground. She had to lower herself to the ground to touch the fringe. Immediately when she touched it, the bleeding stopped. When she lowered herself in humility, God brought healing.

Jesus yelled out over the crowd, *"Who touched me?"* Everybody denied it. But everybody was touching Him. Jesus persisted. What He said tells us a lot about healing.

"But Jesus told him, 'No, someone deliberately touched me, for I felt healing power go out from me.' When the woman realized that Jesus knew, she began to tremble and fell to her knees before him. The whole crowd heard her explain why she had touched him and that she had been immediately healed" (Luke 8:46, 47, NLT).

Jesus knew that this woman needed more than physical healing. She needed all the areas of her life healed. Jesus called her out to restore her reputation and to declare her spiritually clean.

In both Jairus and the bleeding woman, the ingredients for a miracle were present—action, humility and desperation.

An Affirmation of Healing

Jesus approached healing these people in totally different ways, yet He healed them in the same way. The bleeding woman *touched* Jesus. *"Daughter,"* he said to her, *"your faith has made you well. Go in peace"* (Luke 8:48, NLT)

When she touched Jesus she was healed "immediately" (vv. 44, 47). And when He spoke to her, note how He gave her self-esteem and dignity. She is the only woman Jesus ever addressed as "daughter." For twelve years her life had been a curse. Here Jesus blessed her. She could go and experience life at its best.

Jairus' daughter *was touched by* Jesus. Imagine Jairus' frustration. His daughter lay dying. He went to get help. Help was on the way. Then it stopped! Had I been Jairus, I would have probably said, "Jesus, I don't mean to interrupt, but let's go. This woman has been bleeding for twelve years. What's another day? She will be bleeding when you get back. But my daughter will be dead. Come back to her tomorrow. Let's go!" Probably he was chewing on his sandal at this point. Then the news came.

"While he was still speaking to her, a messenger arrived from Jairus's home with the message, 'Your little girl is dead. There's no use troubling the Teacher now'" (Luke 8:49, NLT).

Jesus addressed the frantic thoughts running through Jairus' mind. He said to Jairus, *"Don't be afraid. Just trust me, and she will be all right."* (Luke 8:50, NLT). Jairus' worst fears were realized. But Jesus told him to put away his fears and got at the root of what keeps us from responding to Him—gripping, paralyzing fear. Jesus said, "Don't be afraid." That phrase is used 365 times in the Bible—one for each day of the year. In order to have faith in Jesus, we have to set aside our fear.

Jesus told him, "Just trust me." Jesus called on him for a noble act of faith—to keep on trusting. To us, He says, "Trust me." Jesus gave Jairus a promise straight from God, "She will be all right." To pray with faith means praying according to God's specific and personal promises. Once Jesus did this deep work of faith in Jairus' life, healing his daughter was a piece of cake.

Jesus walked on to Jairus' house. When they arrived, Jesus wouldn't let anyone go in with Him except Peter, James, John and the little girls' father and mother (Luke 8:51). Jesus left the crowd behind, focusing His attention on one need. When Jesus met a need, He did it personally.

The professional mourners had moved into the house—wailing and playing funeral music. But He said, *"'Stop the weeping! She isn't dead; she is only asleep.' But the crowd laughed at him because they all knew she had died"* (Luke 8:52, 53, NLT).

When Jesus came into the room, peace came into the room. *"Then Jesus took her by the hand and said in a loud voice, 'Get up my child!' And at that moment her life returned, and she immediately stood up!"* (Luke 8:54, 55, NLT). Jesus touched her and spoke. A quiet, holy awe covered the room. God was at work!

Heavy Thoughts:

Looking Inside

The power to heal comes from Jesus. Our role is to demonstrate faith. Then He can touch and heal our physical, mental, emotional or spiritual needs. *What needs healing in your life?*

- *Physical*
- *Mental*
- *Emotional*
- *Spiritual*

Ask Jesus to heal you!

Dear Jesus:

Jesus with skin on:

Deliverance!

"The consistent theme of the Bible from the beginning to the end is the conflict between good and evil, between God [Jesus] and the devil. It begins with the serpent in Genesis and ends with the devil in the lake of fire in Revelation 20. The intervening chapters depict the swaying tides of battle in conflict waged in the heavenly sphere as well as on earth."[5]
—Oswald Sanders

Checking It Out

At night he stepped into his parents' room. It was so dark Sean could scarcely make out the two forms sleeping on the waterbed. He aimed at the first form's head and fired. His mother raised up on the other side of the bed and looked to see her son aiming at her forehead. He fired. The prosecution at Sean's trial said he killed "just to watch somebody die."

While both of his parents traveled, Sean Sellers filled the empty hours with the occult. He excelled in the game Dungeons and Dragons. By his senior year he called himself "Ezurate" after the name of the demon he was sure possessed him. Sean prayed at his bedroom altar to Satan, and Ezurate, dressed in black underwear, pulled out the .44 and fired.[6] In your school, people like Sean Sellers walk the halls every day, under the influence of Satan. But yours is not the first generation that has battled against the devil.

"The next day, when they came down from the mountain, a large crowd met him. A man in the crowd called out, 'Teacher, I beg you to look at my son, for he is my only child. A spirit seizes him and he suddenly screams; it throws him into convulsions so that he foams at the mouth. It scarcely ever leaves him and is destroying him'" (Luke 9:37-39).

Hot Notes:

Getting the Point

Read Luke 9:37-43.

Jesus dealt with demons continually. The devil and his demons actively influence our world today as well. Jesus wants us to understand how to turn back the devil and offer deliverance. We discover how as we watch Jesus set this boy free.

The Desperate Father

Jesus and His disciples had just come off a mountaintop experience and into the valley (Luke 9:28-36). When they got there, life's demands pressed in on them.

Mountaintop experiences are great, but people live in the *valley*. In the valley they met the dad and his demon-possessed son. It's in the valley that we will meet people beaten up by Satan who need Jesus' help. Jesus looked beyond the crowd, and totally focused on one boy's problems.

The Demonized Son

Seized by an evil spirit, the son had some terrible consequences in his life: screaming, convulsions, foaming at the mouth, hitting and injuring himself and being constantly harassed. If that happened to this boy and can happen to our friends, then we need to ask ourselves three serious questions:

1. Does the devil really exist?

The devil has many names: Satan, Beelzebub, Lucifer, Prince of the power of the air and others. He talks, thinks and acts. He is the author of death, disease, fear and hatred. He hates God and he hates us. He wants to destroy us and our friends and keep us from God's purpose for our lives. If he can't destroy us, he wants to neutralize us so that we do nothing for God.

Satan comes to us as an "angel of light," not in a red suit with horns and a long tail. He presents everything as attractive and beautiful, but he is seductive and destructive. He wants to outwit us with his clever schemes (2 Corinthians 2:11). Satan is more powerful than we are, but Jesus is more powerful than he is (1 John 4:4).

In case you think this is some weirdo mumbo-jumbo, check this out. Dr. William P. Wilson, M.D., professor of psychiatry at Duke University, said in his diagnosis of some of his patients: "We are left then with only one alternative—they are controlled by an evil spirit."

2. What are demons like?

Demons have characteristics like people—emotions, a mind and will (Mark 5:1-17). Yet they are spirits. They attach themselves to people who are weakened by sin. When we allow a sin to control one part of our lives, then a demon can attach itself. If a demon has attached itself to someone in one generation, that demon can pass on to the next generation (Exodus 34:7).

3. How do demons work?

Demons weave their way into our lives through a variety of ways, such as:
- **Negative emotions.** They can come in through fear, hatred, bitterness and anger.
- **Wrong thinking.** They attach themselves through unbelief, doubt, guilt, confusion, forgetfulness, depression, fantasies, deception, self-condemnation, inferiority and insecurity.
- **Inappropriate use of sex.** They fasten themselves to us through premarital sex, adultery, homosexuality, lust and pornography.
- **Addictions.** They connect through drinking, drugs, smoking, gambling and gluttony.
- **False religions.** They bind themselves to us through cults like Christian Scientism, Jehovah's Witnesses, Mormonism and the New Age.
- **Occult.** They secure themselves through ouija boards, Dungeons and Dragons, horoscopes, voodoo, fortune-telling, astrology, seances, automatic writing, yoga, ESP, reincarnation and occult literature like Edgar Cayce and Jean Dixon.

A demon can attach itself in three different ways:
- **Possession.** A person can be possessed by a demon (like Sean Sellers). Through an open invitation, a demon can come in and possess a person's spirit. Only an unbeliever can be possessed.
- **Obsession.** Through repeated sins or curiosity with the occult, a person can be obsessed. A demon can only attach itself to and influence a person's intellect, emotions or will. This person can be either a believer or an unbeliever.
- **Oppression.** Satan can oppress us when a believer tries to do something significant for Jesus.

Deliverance can come only as we understand how demons work. Only then can we apply the presence and power of Jesus to the situation.

The Defeated Disciples

The demon-possessed boy's situation moved beyond the disciples' ability to handle it. The father said to Jesus, *"I begged your disciples to drive it [the spirit] out, but they could not"* (Luke 9:40). The disciples had forgotten about the authority they had (Luke 9:1).

As Jesus' disciples today, only His authority gives us power over Satan and his demons. That authority can defeat any attack of Satan and deliver ourselves and others.

The Only Deliverer

No incident in the Gospels illustrates the competence of Jesus more clearly. The crowd moved about confused; the father was desperately frustrated; the demons active; the disciples helpless. In walks Jesus! He chided them for their unbelief. *"You stubborn and faithless people,"* Jesus said, *"how long must I be with you and put up with you? Bring him here"* (Luke 9:41, NLT).

He spoke to everyone, but focused on the disciples. So many times they had dealt with this before. They knew they had the authority of Jesus to take care of it, but they forgot and did not use it.

He cast out the demon. *"As the boy came forward, the demon knocked him to the ground and threw him into a violent convulsion. But Jesus rebuked the evil spirit and healed the boy. Then he gave him back to his father. Awe gripped the people as they saw this display of God's power"* (Luke 9:42, 43, NLT).

Jesus handled the situation perfectly. When demonic activity swirls around us, we can follow what Jesus did:

- **Jesus rebuked the evil spirit.**
  Using instructions from other parts of the New Testament, we can do what Jesus did by taking Jesus' authority and saying: "In the name of Jesus and by His shed blood on the cross, I rebuke you. . . ."
- **Jesus restored the boy.**
  Just as Jesus brought the child to wholeness (physically, mentally, spiritually and socially), we need to pray for people we think are under demonic influences so that they will be delivered.
- **Jesus returned the boy to his father.**
  Jesus not only cast out the demon, He brought their family back together. Home is Hell when someone is attacked by Satan. Knowing that, we can pray for their family and meet with their family to bring them together around Christ.
- **Jesus reflected the awesome power of God.**
  When people see us humbly pray for people and boldly deal with issues and problems in our friends' lives, people will be amazed at the greatness of God.

Heavy Thoughts:

Looking Inside

Understanding the demonic world and Jesus' authority over it, we can see how Satan can affect us and our friends. But Jesus wants us to boldly step up and, like Him, push back the kingdom of Satan and bring in the kingdom of Jesus. Deliverance will come to others as we act on the authority and power of Jesus.

Dear Jesus:

Jesus with skin on:

The Big Investment

"They were not theologians or political leaders—just ordinary men who became extraordinary under the molding hand of the Master Potter. That makes His selection of them the more wonderful."[7]
—*J. Oswald Sanders*

Checking It Out

If we take a calculator and add a series of numbers, they look like this: 2 + 2 = 4; 4 + 4 = 8; 8 + 8 = 16; 16 + 16 = 32; 32 + 32 = 64. Multiply these numbers and they present a much different picture: 2 x 2 = 4; 4 x 4 = 16; 16 x 16 = 256; 256 x 256 = 65,536. If you turned those numbers into dollar bills, which approach would you prefer?

If these numbers represented people to influence for Christ and if they multiplied one number per year, in 32 years all five billion people in the world would be reached. Jesus was brilliant! He knew math. Instead of choosing to stay on earth and do all of His work Himself, He chose to invest in and multiply His life through His disciples.

"One day as Jesus was walking along the shores of the Sea of Galilee, he saw Simon and his brother, Andrew, fishing with a net. . . . Jesus called out to them, 'Come, be my disciples, and I will show you how to fish for people.' And they left their nets at once and went with him" (Mark 1:16-18, NLT).

Hot Notes:

Getting the Point

Read Mark 1:16-18; Matthew 10:2-4; and Matthew 28:18-20.

Jesus had a plan! He invested in twelve people's lives—in depth. His goal was to give the enterprise to them and turn them loose to change the world. How did He do that? And how do we fit into that plan?

Picking Ordinary People

Jesus knew people and He understood leadership. So why did He pick the people He did? Almost all were young, some were teenagers. They were so . . . ordinary!

- **Simon Peter** could have been known as "Big Mouth." He seemed to choose every day which foot to stick in his mouth. Once Peter promised Jesus that if everybody else denied Him, he would not. He swore he would stick with Jesus. But a seventh-grade servant girl accused him of being one of Jesus' disciples, and Peter denied Jesus for the third time in a matter of minutes.
- **Andrew** (Peter's brother) did some good things like bringing Peter to Jesus, bringing five loaves and two fish to feed 5,000 people and bringing some Greeks to Jesus. Bringing Peter was a big deal, but the other two weren't. He brought the boy's lunch because he was hungry. And the Greeks came to him. All he had to say was, "Jesus is right over there." Andrew lived in Peter's shadow.
- **James and John** (sons of Zebedee) had the nicknames "the Sons of Thunder." Walking through

Samaria one day, they met some people who had rejected Jesus. Love burst forth from their hearts and they said, "Let's bring down fire from heaven and burn 'em up!" Another time John found that some people were baptizing in Jesus' name. John got mad and said to Jesus, "Do you want James and me to go over and take care of 'em?"

- **Philip** was spiritually dense. When Jesus fed the 5000, He turned to Philip by name and said, "How are we going to feed them?" Philip: "Well, let's see . . . if we had 200 days' pay, we wouldn't have enough to give everybody a crumb." Philip didn't get it. He had already seen Jesus heal the blind, the deaf, the lame and raise up dead people!
- **Bartholomew** is virtually unknown. Some think he was Nathanael. Jesus respected him for his pure motives (John 1:47).
- **Thomas** has the rap of being the doubter. In spite of his doubt, he became a loyal believer. When Jesus heard that Lazarus was sick, he went to Bethany. The disciples got mad. They knew if Jesus went there, He (and they) would be killed. They tried to talk Jesus out of it. But Thomas said, "Men, if he is going to die, let's go die with Him."
- **Matthew** was a tax collector who became a disciple. He wrote the book of Matthew. He threw a big party so Jesus could meet his buddies.
- **James, the son of Alphaeus** is not mentioned elsewhere besides who his father was. That's all. In three years of hanging out with Jesus, the Bible records not one thing about James.
- **Thaddaeus** may have also been named Judas (not Iscariot). We don't even know his dad's name! Zero. Zip. In John 14:22, he asked, *"But, Lord, why do you intend to show yourself to us and not to the world?"* Exit Judas. That's the last we hear of him.
- **Simon the Zealot** belonged to a political party called Zealots. His ultraright-wing friends had determined to get rid of Rome. Their party engaged in guerrilla warfare—cloak and dagger stuff. They killed Roman soldiers in the night. In three years the Bible never mentioned his zeal. Actually, not one word is recorded about him.
- **Judas Iscariot** was the keeper of the moneybag. He may be best known because of his betrayal of Jesus with a kiss, then his subsequent suicide by hanging.

This picture of the disciples isn't flattering. Clearly Jesus picked very ordinary people to follow Him. Then for three years they didn't do much to contribute to the cause. But Jesus did choose them. And the further along He went in His ministry, the more time He spent with them. What did He have in mind?

Planning with a Purpose

How did Jesus spend His time with the disciples for three years to prepare them for the task of making disciples of all nations?

• He let the disciples watch Him serve.

Jesus never asked His disciples to do something He was not willing to do Himself. He let the life of His Father flow through Him to love and serve people every day. Jesus took His disciples with Him every place He went. When He taught, they listened. When He healed the sick and delivered people from demons, they watched. When He reached out with compassion to people, they could feel the love. They saw it all—and learned by watching.

• The disciples did it and He was with them.

Jesus sent His disciples from village to village to practice what they had seen Him do—teaching, healing, delivering, loving (Mark 6:7-13). When they succeeded, Jesus helped them process it. When they failed, He stuck with them. When they operated in His power, they were successful. They weren't ready to turn the world upside down yet, but they had come a long way from the fishing boats and tax tables.

• **They did it and He was in the background to encourage.**

Over three years Jesus let them try everything. They knew the thrill of casting out demons. They experienced the persecution of the religious leaders. They hurt deeply when Jesus was crucified. In all of this, He remained with them. Then, Jesus ascended into Heaven with the promise that more was to come.

Profiting from the Investment

Through the process of making disciples, Jesus showed them how ordinary they were. Then He showed them how extraordinary *He* was through the cross and resurrection. Then Jesus sent His Spirit to empower them and they set out to change the world. And they did!

Peter, the blabbermouth, became the leader. After leading the church in Jerusalem, he was martyred upside down on a cross because he knew he was not worthy to die like his Master did. James, one Son of Thunder, became a martyr. John, the other Son of Thunder, became the apostle of love, exiled on an island for the cause of Christ.

The other disciples became extraordinary leaders in the church. Thomas, for example, took the gospel to India. Of the other disciples, three were crucified, three were stoned, one was shot through with arrows and one was run through with a sword.

In a few short years they, and those they discipled, and the ones they discipled, and the ones they discipled took the message of Jesus to the entire known world. That's multiplication at its best!

Heavy Thoughts:

Looking Inside

Like the disciples, we are very ordinary people. Through the discipling process we understand how extraordinary Jesus is. With the Holy Spirit, we become extraordinary like Him.

In what ways are you ordinary? In what ways has Jesus made you extraordinary?

Who is discipling you? Who are you discipling?

When we pursue becoming disciples and disciplers, it will be said of us and our generation,

"These [people] who have turned the world upside down have come here also" (Acts 17:6, RSV).

Dear Jesus:

Jesus with skin on:

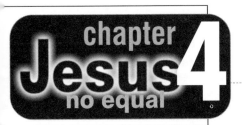

Bridging the Gap

The prisoner stood without speaking as the soldiers stripped him to the waist, tied his hands together and bent his body across a rail. One of the soldiers picked up a whip made of leather strands into which bits of metal or bone had been tied at the ends. Then began the ordeal commonly called "the halfway death," so called because it was intended to bring the victim just short of dying.

It was a form of torture peculiar to the Romans. The Jews did it differently. Their law limited flogging to a maximum of 39 strikes of the whip. But the Romans had no such rule. They flogged till the man doing the whipping got so tired he couldn't go on.

After the flogging, his back flayed open like a newly plowed field, the prisoner was led to the palace of the Roman governor. A company of soldiers, perhaps as many as 600, had gathered. They draped a purple robe, symbol of royalty, around the prisoner's shredded back so that the blood, as it coagulated, stuck to the fabric.

Someone had broken a branch from a thornbush and fastened the ends together to form a "crown." The soldiers placed it on the victim's head, jabbing the long thorns into his scalp. To complete the mockery, the soldiers struck his head with a rod, spit on him and bowed down to him shouting, "Hail, king of the Jews!"

The prisoner reeled, half-conscious, before the jeering soldiers. A day of unimaginable punishment had just begun for the prisoner they called Jesus of Nazareth.

Place of the Skull

That same morning, a hideous procession wound its way through the crowded streets of Jerusalem. A heavy wooden beam had been lifted onto Jesus' bruised and bleeding shoulders. Weak from blood loss, pain, hunger and lack of sleep, He stumbled forward. He carried on His back what was to form the horizontal beam of His cross.

Somewhere along the way, Jesus stumbled and fell. A man named Simon happened to be passing by, and the soldiers forced him to carry the crossbeam.

When the procession reached Golgotha, a hill known as "the Place of the Skull," the soldiers nailed Jesus to a cross. They hammered a spike through each wrist, between the two long bones of the forearms. Next, they nailed His feet to the cross. Jesus' flesh ripped as the soldiers stood the cross upright and dropped its base into a hole in the ground.

By three o'clock that afternoon, Jesus' crucifixion, an ordeal which the Roman historian Cicero called "the most horrible torture ever devised by man," had ended. The man who claimed to be the Son of God was dead. And the question screaming in the minds of His followers was, "Why?" Why had it happened?

To understand the answer, we move ahead in time some 2,000 years to an isolated spot in the American Rockies. Five teenagers, ranging in age from 15 to 18, stand looking over a cliff.

They are backpackers. Nearing the end of a three-day hike, their path has been blocked by a canyon, some 100 feet deep and 30 feet wide. Since the five know of no other way to reach their destination, they begin trying, one by one, to cross the canyon.

Making It on His Own

The first hiker to try crossing is Alex Athlete. Alex is tall, with muscles rippling all over his body. He's considered the big jock on campus. Nobody can match him in athletic skill or strength. Alex has a philosophy about life that goes something like this: "I'm a winner. I've got what it takes. I can do it because I try harder."

Alex does 25 sit-ups and 25 push-ups to get warmed up for the jump. He puts on his $150 jumping shoes and starts his approach run. By most standards, Alex's jump is impressive. He makes it about 28 feet, but not far enough to get across. He crashes to the bottom of the canyon. Splat!

Faked Out by Her Brain

If Alex couldn't make it, perhaps another of the five hikers can—maybe Brandi Brain. Brandi is so clever in math that it doesn't take her long, with her pocket slide rule and her book of logarithmic tables (which she always carries backpacking), to figure out that the canyon is 30 feet, 3⅝ inches across.

She also knows her exact body weight. So, according to the laws of velocity and momentum, Brandi computes exactly how fast she needs to run, exactly what the wind resistance is, exactly how far and at what angle she has to jump to get across safely.

But something—perhaps only Brandi could figure out exactly what—goes wrong. Despite her calculations, she makes it only 16 feet, 5⅜ inches. Brandi joins Alex at the bottom of the canyon. Splat!

Where Money Fails

Monty Moneybags is next in line, and he looks a little worried. That's unusual. Monty has never had to worry about anything. He's always had enough money to take care of most problems. All he's had to do is call Mom, and she'd come running with the car or the checkbook, or whatever else it was Monty wanted.

Monty's money has opened a lot of doors for him, but when it comes to crossing the canyon, he does no better than his two friends. Monty buys the best jumping equipment money can buy, but that doesn't do the job. He ends up on the bottom with Alex and Brandi. Splat!

Popularity at Any Price

With their three fellow hikers lying lifeless at the bottom of the cliff, you'd think the other two backpackers would turn back. But not Calvin Clone, who's next in line. Calvin always follows the crowd. If the other guys smoke, so does Calvin. If they get drunk, he does too. If they fry their brains on dope, Calvin joins right in. If they go to church, he goes too.

The other guys had jumped, so Calvin thinks over the situation—for about two seconds—then takes the plunge. So long, Calvin.

"Good Guys" Finish Last

The wind is really whipping down the mountainside now. The last hiker, Rachel Religious, pulls her jacket around her as she considers her predicament. Rachel has always had answers for everything—pat answers, perhaps, but answers. She proves almost every Sunday what a good girl she is. (The rest of the week doesn't count, in Rachel's way of thinking.)

Rachel's also active in her youth group. She's fairly certain that all her churchgoing will "pay off" when she takes her turn at the jump. What Rachel doesn't know is that she's no better off than Alex Athlete, who trusted in his physical strength; or Brandi Brain, who trusted in her brains; or Monty Moneybags, who trusted in his money; or Calvin Clone, who relied on his friends. Being a "good girl" might impress a lot of people, but not 30-foot canyons. Rachel joins her friends at the bottom. Splat!

The Wide Gap

So, what does this little make-believe tragedy have to do with why Jesus died? Let the mountainside canyon represent the gap that exists between God and humans. Then let the efforts of Alex, Brandi, Monty, Calvin and Rachel stand for human efforts to bridge the gap. And you begin to see the connection.

A tremendous gap stands between God and us, between His holiness and our selfishness. If we could see the holiness and absolute purity of God, we would understand how sinful we are and the difficulty involved in bridging the gap. We would understand why it's impossible for us to bridge the gap on our own.

The Old Testament prophet Isaiah saw in a vision a glimpse of God sitting on His throne in Heaven. Just a glimpse was all Isaiah needed to realize how sinful he was. *"'Woe to me!' he cried, 'I am ruined!'"* (Isaiah 6:5).

When Simon Peter realized that Jesus was God's Son, he said almost the same thing: *"Go away from me, Lord; I am a sinful man!"* (Luke 5:8).

What Peter had to learn is this: *God is holy, but He is also love.* He proved that love by offering His Son to die on the cross. A 30-foot canyon is nothing compared to the wide gap which God's love and holiness had to span to reach us sinful humans.

Money can open doors. It can buy the "right" kinds of clothes. But it can't make anyone right with God. Ditto for physical strength, and brainpower—and even being a "good girl." People can't buy or earn what God alone is able to give.

Expensive Bridge Building

Peter wrote, *"For Christ died for sins once for all, the righteous for the unrighteous, to bring you to God"* (1 Peter 3:18). *"He himself bore our sins in his body on the tree, so that we might die to sins and live for righteousness"* (1 Peter 2:24). God bridged the gap. But what a cost!

Because salvation is free as far as man's part is concerned, we could get the impression that it didn't cost anything. But one look at Jesus on the cross shows what a tremendous price God paid. If we saw a realistic picture of Jesus' death, it would be too gross to look at. And yet, the spiritual pain Jesus experienced on the cross was even greater than His physical pain.

Why did He allow it? Simple. He went through that pain so that you and I wouldn't have to go through it. Two statements Jesus made while on the cross help explain this reality:

1. "My God, my God, why have you forsaken Me?" (Matthew 27:46).

As Jesus hung in agony on the cross, God the Father turned His back. For the first time ever, Jesus was totally separated from His Father's presence—flung to the bottom of the canyon, going through Hell so you and I wouldn't have to.

At this point Jesus took on Himself all of our sin—the garbage in our lives. As a result, His fellowship with God the Father was broken. Think about the sinful things you've done. And realize that God's Son was forsaken by His Father in order to take care of your sin problem. Unbelievable!

It's impossible for us to fully understand how much it cost Jesus to bridge the gap. But understand this: He did it for you.

2. "It is finished" (John 19:30).

This final statement of Jesus on the cross was not a confession of defeat, but of victory. The canyon had been bridged! Jesus had paid the full price for mankind's sin and selfishness. Because of that payment, you and I can be totally forgiven and accepted by God. *"If we confess our sins, he is faithful and just and will forgive us our sins and purify us from all unrighteousness"* (1 John 1:9).

Not only did Jesus' death provide forgiveness, it also provided freedom from guilt: *"Therefore, there is now no condemnation for those who are in Christ Jesus"* (Romans 8:1).

Not only was sin forgiven and guilt taken away, but the curse of death was broken. The story doesn't end with Jesus' death. Three days later He burst out of the grave.

I learned a dramatic lesson in the meaning of Jesus' resurrection when a high school friend was dying of cancer. This friend, with whom I had run track, had shriveled to 96 pounds. I visited him in the hospital and then talked with his mother. "Barry," she asked me, "where is God?"

At that moment, I had no answer. Then I realized, *He's in the same place He was 2,000 years ago when His own Son was dying*. For the first time, I really understood that in Jesus Christ the sting of death is removed. Jesus finished off death!

Toward the end of the movie *Ben Hur*, the camera focuses on the cross, then on Jesus' feet. Blood and rain drip down His legs and fall into a puddle below the cross. The puddle turns red. Then it overflows and runs down the hill. The hill slowly turns red. Finally, the blood flows into a river which turns red, then into the ocean—it too turns red. The scene symbolizes the fact that Jesus died for the whole world.

He died for His critics and enemies who stood gloating that day because they'd managed to see Him killed. He died for the bystanders who really didn't care about Him one way or the other. He died for the small group of His followers who stood beneath the cross watching Him die. And He died for you and me.

Up Close and Personal

1. *Name one person you know who fits the description of Alex Athlete, Brandi Brain, Monty Moneybags, Calvin Clone or Rachel Religious in the backpacker story. Which character are you most like?*

2. *Think about the reason for the wide gap between God and us. Describe how helpless you are to bridge that gap yourself.*

3. *These verses tell what Jesus' death did for us in bridging the gap. Carefully look over each one so you can see why it was so important for Jesus to bridge the gap for you:*
   * *1 John 1:9*

   * *Romans 8:1*

   * *John 11:25, 26*

Not too sure about that last verse? Keep reading.

The Death of Jesus

The Agony of Victory

"What was the struggle, exactly? Fear of pain and death? Of course. Jesus no more relished the prospects than you or I do. But there was more at work as well; a new experience for Jesus that can only be called God-forsakenness. At its core Gethsemane depicts, after all, the story of an unanswered prayer. The cup of suffering was not removed."[1]
—Philip Yancey

Checking It Out

Every Saturday afternoon I would watch it. For about sixty seconds the TV sports program would show athletes in different sports jumping, scoring, winning. Then with athletes falling, hurting, failing, the final clip showed a skier come off a long, high jump, crash into the ramp, fly into space, skid for fifty yards, and then lie in a pile. The announcer would proclaim, "The thrill of victory . . . and the agony of defeat."

Jesus was in Jerusalem knowing that hostile religious people wanted to kill Him. A woman poured perfume over His feet in preparation for His death. He ate the final meal together with His disciples. Judas left to betray Him. Then Jesus took His disciples about three-fourths of a mile outside Jerusalem to the beautiful estate of a wealthy man, surrounded by a stone wall.

Let's go to the Garden of Gethsemane now and get in step with Jesus as we walk with Him to the cross. If you have felt overwhelmed by circumstances, deserted by your friends or betrayed by someone you thought cared about you, then this is for you. It's not a pity party. It's not "the agony of defeat." Rather you will discover in Jesus the agony of victory.

"He withdrew about a stone's throw beyond them, knelt down and prayed, 'Father, if you are willing, take this cup from me; yet not my will, but yours be done.' . . . And being in anguish, he prayed more earnestly, and his sweat was like drops of blood falling to the ground" (Luke 22:41, 42, 44).

Hot Notes:

Ⓖetting the Point

Read Mark 14:32-42.

Jesus was facing the greatest crisis of His life—His own private agony. He was in deep distress. Jesus told His disciples, *"Sit here while I go and pray."* He took Peter, James and John with Him. At that moment *"he began to be filled with horror and deep distress"* (v. 33, NLT). What does this mean? What did He see?

He saw the "horror" of taking on the sin of the world. Here it hit Him full force. He had a feeling of terrified surprise so great that probably His hair stood on end and His skin began to crawl. He knew what was about to happen. When He saw it in the garden, it scared Him to death, literally. He told His disciples, *"My soul is crushed with grief to the point of death"* (v. 34, NLT).

Then He saw His Father. "Deep distress" literally means "not at home." Seeing the sin and the cross in front of Him, it caused Jesus to be homesick. Jesus so longed to be back in the total presence of His Father, it created serious stress. The result of this horror and stress was so great that His sweat fell to the ground like great drops of blood (Luke 22:44). According to Bill Counts in his book *Once a Carpenter*, medically this is known as *haematridrosos*. Under extreme emotional stress, blood vessels expand so much that they break when they come in contact with sweat glands. The person then literally sweats blood.

No one in history ever struggled as Jesus did in the garden. But it was there that Jesus won the victory over Himself. What gauntlet did He have to pass through to experience this "agony of victory"?

The "Hour"

This was the time in God's plan when He had to suffer and die for sin. Jesus knew this hour was coming. He knew that going through it was the purpose for which He came to this earth (John 12:23-28). Right here He made the final decision to go to the cross. His humanity resisted that hour. He was no puppet on a string. He did not want this. This stands far and above as the greatest test of obedience to His Father. If the answer is "no," He can still go back. If the answer is "yes," then the cross waits for Him.

The "Cup"

The cup represented His fiercest temptation to back out. As He looked into it, He must have asked, "Is there another way?" He did not want to die at the young age of 33 under any circumstances. He knew about the physical pain of crucifixion and He shuddered at the thought of it. But even more severe was the agony of bearing the sin and guilt of a lost world. What tempted Him to back away the most was the separation He would experience from His Father.

The "Will"

In the end Jesus asked His Father one simple question: "Is there any way to do this other than for Me to die on the cross?" His whole being cringed at the thought of the cross. But He cringed even more at the thought of not doing His Father's will. In the end there was victory! He said, *"Yet not what I will, but what you will"* (Mark 14:36).

In addition to dealing with His deep distress, Jesus endured the desertion of friends. In times of trouble we want someone with us. They don't need to do or say anything—just be there. Having friends there gives us the strength to endure. But Jesus had to endure the flight of His friends. When He needed them most, they fell asleep—three times (Mark 14:37, 40, 41). The tension had drained them. They wanted to help, but they just did not have the strength to do it. Jesus realized that He had to face this ordeal alone. Emotionally, He pushed through it and told them, "Up, let's be going." Again victory.

Finally, He withstood the disloyalty of Judas. For three years Jesus had invested every hour of every day in Judas. Then Judas stabbed Him in the back, or to be more accurate, kissed Him on the cheek

(Mark 14:43-52).

A crowd of 400 to 700 swarmed on Jesus, led by Judas. He had been a busy boy. He made himself available to Caiaphas, the high priest, to give away Jesus' whereabouts. Caiaphas gathered the temple police, pulled some political strings and took a squad of Roman soldiers. Judas led them all to the garden.

In the dim torchlight the soldiers knew they would need a definite indication of whom to arrest. Judas, already having made some horrible decisions, made another one. He chose the kiss. A kiss was a sign of respect and affection. When he kissed Jesus, it was not an ordinary kiss, but an intense kiss of affection, which made his act more despicable.

In the middle of the chaos, Jesus was the picture of calmness. The soldiers had come to arrest Him, but He was in control. He put the ear back on a soldier. And He gave God's perspective to what was happening when He made the statement, *"But the Scriptures must be fulfilled"* (Mark 14:49). And they would be! Victory reigned in the midst of the agony!

Heavy Thoughts:

Looking Inside

In the deepest, darkest crisis of His life, Jesus didn't experience defeat, but victory.

What kind of crisis have you been through? Like Jesus, have you ever been overwhelmed by the circumstances, abandoned by your friends or deserted by someone you thought cared about you? Maybe all three! In Jesus, you have what you need to experience "the agony of victory."

Dear Jesus:

Jesus with skin on:

Disorder in the Court

"The might of the world, the most sophisticated religious system of its time allied with the most powerful political empire, arrays itself against a solitary figure, the only perfect man who has ever lived. Though he is mocked by the powers . . . the Gospels give the strong, ironic sense that he himself is overseeing the whole, long process. . . . Now, as death nears, he calls the shots."[2]
—*Philip Yancey*

Checking It Out

They placed handcuffs on Tommy, shoved him into the police car, then locked him up in jail. They accused my friend and fellow minister of making threatening calls to a woman. Bail was posted. A lawyer was selected. He was arraigned and the trial was set that could send him to prison for years.

Total injustice had been done. First, Tommy is so kind he was not capable of the crime. Secondly, the police had only very sparse circumstantial evidence. Thirdly, and weirdest of all, the lawyer hired a private detective, and through a bizarre series of events he found out that a woman who barely knew Tommy was disguising her voice as a man and making the threatening calls, then blaming it on Tommy. It took five months to get this gross injustice untangled and out of the courts.

And that is only kid's stuff compared to the injustice Jesus went through when He went before the high priest and the Sanhedrin. If you have ever been through an injustice, like Tommy, you can know that Jesus has already been there before you.

"The chief priests and the whole Sanhedrin were looking for evidence against Jesus so that they could put him to death, but they did not find any. Many testified falsely against him, but their statements did not agree" (Mark 14:55, 56).

Hot Notes:

Getting the Point

Read the whole account in Mark 14:53-65.

Jesus almost died from a nervous breakdown in the garden. Judas betrayed Him with a kiss. His friends deserted Him. The soldiers arrested Him. He faced an unjust trial. There was disorder in the court.

Falsely Accused

In order to bring charges against Jesus, His enemies had to go through a series of illegal steps.

- **They took Jesus to the high priest (verse 53).**

  The high priest was the leading Jewish religious and political leader. The one in office at this time was

Caiaphas. But he was only a puppet to his father-in-law Annas. Annas had been the high priest for sixteen years. Then five of his sons had held the position. At this time Caiaphas held the position and Annas held the power. You might call it a family-controlled business.

Annas hated Jesus. Why? A very wealthy Jew, he operated a booth in the temple where he sold animals for sacrifice at a marked-up price, then he pocketed the proceeds. When Jesus tore up the temple and drove out the businesses, Annas's business was one of them. Not only was he humiliated, he lost money. He wanted a piece of Jesus and Jesus would stand trial before him.

- **They led Jesus before the Sanhedrin (verse 53).**
Evidently, after Annas got through with Jesus, he called a meeting of these seventy Jewish leaders. They were like the Jewish supreme court. They ruled Israel, but were limited in their power by Rome. One thing they did not have, the power to inflict the death penalty.

The Sanhedrin had a real dilemma. How could they put Jesus to death? Since they could not inflict the death penalty, they concocted a plan to assemble a fast trial with phony charges, get a guilty verdict, then bring Jesus to Pilate before morning to get him to issue the death penalty.

- **They tried Jesus illegally (verse 55).**
The Sanhedrin had certain regulations that had to be met before they could call a meeting officially:
1. A criminal case had to be tried in the daytime and completed in the daytime.
2. No trial could be held during the Passover.
3. Only a "not guilty" verdict could be finished on the same day it started.
4. No meeting was valid unless they met in the official meeting place, "the Hall of Hewn Stone."
5. All evidence had to be verified by two witnesses examined separately. Giving a false witness was
 punishable by death.

Not one of these regulations was followed. The trial was illegal before it even started. To add insult to injury, the trial was supposed to begin with the witnesses for the accused. Can you imagine if the trial had been a fair one? "I was blind . . . now I see." "I was lame . . . now I walk." "I was deaf . . . now I hear." "I was dead . . . now I'm alive." But they did not do that.

Then the court was to present the evidence against the accused. The Sanhedrin had worked overtime on this, but they were not supposed to be the prosecutors. Their role was to function as the jury. But they were so anxious to get Jesus convicted, they looked long and hard for evidence to present against Him. They couldn't find any, so they got some people to accuse Him falsely. To give a false witness was so serious that the witnesses were told when they took the stand: "Forget not, O witness, in this trial for life, if you sin, the blood of the accused and the blood of his seed unto the end of time shall be imputed unto you." That legal talk says simply, "You lie and you're as good as dead."

Not only did they break the rules, they looked stupid because they could not even get two of the witnesses to agree. What a joke!

Questions and Answers

Annas could see that the trial was falling apart right in front of his eyes. So he took things into his own hands. He did several things to bring the trial to a quick end. He "stood up." That put him above Jesus so he could verbally attack Him and look down on Him. He asked intimidating questions. Jesus refused to answer. He asked Jesus point-blank, *"Are you the Christ, the Son of the Blessed One?"* (v. 61). Again, foul play. He was not allowed to ask a question in which the accused could incriminate himself.

The high priest alone had the power to put a defendant under oath before God. Annas did this, knowing if Jesus answered this honestly, He would condemn Himself. The pressure was on. If ever there was a time to lie, this was it. This was the crucial moment—all of the universe held its breath. If Jesus answered "no," He would walk out a free man. But if He answered "yes," He would be saying He is deity—and sign His own death warrant.

Jesus gave a two-part answer. He responded "*I am.*" He could have stopped there, and, meekly gone to the cross. Not the Lion. He quoted Daniel 7:13 and proclaimed the ultimate triumph of the Messiah: He will sit at God's right hand and He will come on the clouds of Heaven in power as the conquering Messiah. At the lowest slime pit of injustice, Jesus ruled in one of the greatest moments of His life!

Beaten Up by the Jury

As much as they wanted Jesus to condemn Himself, when He did, it hit a raw nerve. The high priest tore his robe. (He was required to do that if he heard blasphemy.) He thought what Jesus said was blasphemy—irreverence for God—because He didn't fit the mold of what they thought the Messiah would be like.

Because of what Jesus said, they felt free to let all of their hostility toward Jesus come out. They spit on Him. To spit in another person's face is totally humiliating. They struck Him with their fists. Mocking Him, they came up with a cruel version of "blind man's bluff." They blindfolded Him, then punched Him in the face. "Prophesy! Who hit you?" they said.

Then they turned Him over to the temple guards. They ganged up on Him, while He was still blindfolded, and beat Him up. Jesus' face and body were swollen and covered with blood, sweat and spit.

Heavy Thoughts:

Looking Inside

The most law-abiding citizen in history was condemned to die in a court of law. Disorder in the court brought about total injustice.

When did you last say, "That's not fair!"? Life is not fair. If someone treats you unjustly, how should you respond to it?

Dear Jesus:

Jesus with skin on:

By Unpopular Demand

"I have marveled at, and sometimes openly questioned, the self-restraint God has shown throughout history, allowing the Genghis Khans and the Hitlers and the Stalins to have their way. But nothing—nothing—compares to the self-restraint shown that dark Friday in Jerusalem."[3]
—*Philip Yancey*

Checking It Out

Some people encouraged me to run for president of the student body in high school. So I did. We had all the usual campaign speeches and debates. But the morning of the election, as I walked to class, posters plastered all over the campus called for my defeat. And these signs carried the signatures of people who were supposed to be my friends! When I got a copy of the school paper a few minutes later, one whole page contained a smear campaign against me. The editor, who lived next door to me, was often sick and I had taken care of him many nights when no one else would. He led the campaign against me. The negative campaigning caused the vote to swing to my opponent. I lost. And I learned a valuable lesson: popularity is fleeting and people will turn against you in a heartbeat!

In a much more vicious manner, people who had hung around Jesus turned against Him. First the council, then Pilate and the crowd cast a nasty negative vote against a very unpopular Jesus. They sent Him to the cross—by unpopular demand!

"'What shall I do, then, with the one you call the king of the Jews?' Pilate asked them.
'Crucify him!' they shouted.
'Why? What crime has he committed?' asked Pilate.
But they shouted all the louder, 'Crucify him!'
Wanting to satisfy the crowd, Pilate released Barabbas to them. He had Jesus flogged, and handed him over to be crucified" (Mark 15:12-15).

Hot Notes:

Getting the Point

Read the account of Jesus before Pontius Pilate in Mark 15:1-15.

Slowly the light began to break over Jerusalem that Friday morning. The holiday tourists had just begun to stir. While they woke up, Jesus had been up—all night. After the ordeal with Annas and after the soldiers had finished abusing Him, they locked Him in a room in the house of Caiaphas for about three hours. Exhausted and aching from the beating and lack of sleep, Jesus was taken through one more illegal maneuver. Jesus' worst nightmare still lay ahead of Him.

The Last Hurdle

The Sanhedrin held a consultation and "reached a decision" (v. 1). Knowing a capital punishment trial could not be held at night, and knowing 24 hours had to pass before a sentencing, the Sanhedrin already had decided to wait until morning to legalize the illegal action they had taken the night before. They knew they had to get Him to Pilate early in the morning. Jesus didn't say a word. They handed Him over to Pilate, the last hurdle to clear in order to put Jesus to death. As the only person in Jerusalem who could deliver the death sentence, Pilate controlled Jesus' fate.

As governor of Judea, Pilate answered only to Caesar. To become governor he had to prove himself a strong warrior, a skillful leader and a clever administrator. He was decisive, unbending, ruthless and savage—and he hated the Jews. He lived up the road in Caesarea, but came to Jerusalem only during the Passover to keep the hotheaded Jews under control. He did not usually handle them with velvet gloves. But Pilate had trouble on his hands. He began his administration making a serious blunder. He used the temple treasury to pay for the repair of a Roman aqueduct, which supplied the water to Jerusalem. The Jews demonstrated and Pilate killed some of them. The Jews hated him. His job was in jeopardy. Tension filled the air.

The Trumped-Up Charges

The Jews had charged Jesus with blasphemy, a religious charge. They knew that would not stand up with Pilate. He despised religious squabbles. So they tweaked the charges.

They said, *"We have found this man subverting our nation. He opposes payment of taxes to Caesar and claims to be Christ, a king"* (Luke 23:2).

Everyone knew the charges were a lie. The first two were pretty vague, but the third one grabbed Pilate's attention—*a king!* Jewish zealots constantly plotted against Rome. He knew that a claim to be king in the Roman Empire was treason. Pilate knew that if he did not investigate he would lose his job.

That's why he asked Jesus, *"Are you the king of the Jews?"*

"'Yes, it is as you say,' Jesus replied" (Mark 15:2).

Pilate and the Jews went back and forth, arguing with each other. Finally Pilate brought the conversation back to Jesus: *"Aren't you going to answer?"* (Mark 15:4).

Why Jesus' silence? There was nothing to be said! All lines of communication had broken down.

The Fickle Crowd

Was this the same crowd that had laid palm branches at Jesus' feet in worship only a few days before? If so, how did they turn on Jesus so quickly? No, this was a different crowd. Jesus' supporters knew He had been arrested, but had no idea He would go to trial so quickly. Gathering supporters of Barabbas and the crowd who had come to visit the city, the religious leaders turned the crowd on Jesus and Pilate. Pilate was left pleading and shouting. He had lost all control (Mark 15:8, 11, 15).

Substitute for Barabbas

At the time of the Passover Feast, the Romans had a custom of releasing a Jewish prisoner—whoever the people wanted and no matter what the crime. Pilate knew Jesus had not committed a crime.

Pilate pulled the "Barabbas Trick" out of the bag in order to free Jesus and save his own neck. He selected the most disgusting criminal and then asked the crowd to choose between the two. Barabbas had committed a murder as a radical revolutionary. Probably he belonged to a zealot band called Sicarii ("dagger bearers"), a violent, fanatical group who carried their daggers beneath their cloaks and assassinated Romans. He thought they would choose Jesus because He was popular with the people. He should have known better (Mark 15:6-8).

Held in the Fortress of Antonia, Barabbas could hear the crowds yelling, but he could not hear the words of Pilate. Listen to what Barabbas heard: *"'Do you want me to release to you the king of the Jews?' asked Pilate. . . . But the chief priests stirred up the crowd to have Pilate release Barabbas instead. 'What shall I do, then, with the one you call the king of the Jews?' Pilate asked them.*

'Crucify him!' they shouted.

'Why? What crime has he committed?' asked Pilate.

But they shouted all the louder, 'Crucify him!'" (Mark 15:9-14).

Barabbas panicked. He knew he was a dead man. Expecting the soldiers to come and take him to the site of his execution, to his surprise, they released him! He was the one intended for the cross! He deserved death! But Jesus took his place!

The Final Cruelty

Pilate chose to satisfy the crowd rather than do what he knew was right. He gave in to the pressure in order to remain popular. He made a bad choice.

To make matters worse, he handed Jesus over to be flogged. What happened next ranked right up with the cross in its cruelty. Called "the scourge," flogging was gruesome and tortuous. They bent Jesus over and tied Him to a post, exposing His back. Then they beat Him with a "cat of nine tails," which consisted of nine straps of leather with lead tips on the end. The Romans allowed a person to take as many blows as the "lictor" wanted to give. They called it "the halfway death" because many died or went crazy before they made it to the cross. The Jews allowed a person to take only 39 hits. The Romans beat Jesus beyond recognition.

Heavy Thoughts:

Looking Inside

The religious leaders got their way. Pilate wondered about Jesus, then waffled. The crowd screamed, *"Crucify him!"* Barabbas was set free because of Him. And Jesus Himself was sentenced to the cross as a substitute. How appropriate! Barabbas represents us. Like Barabbas, we are guilty and condemned. Before God, we deserve death. Jesus willingly took our place on the cross.

"For God made Christ, who never sinned, to be the offering for our sin, so that we could be made right with God through Christ" (2 Corinthians 5:21, NLT).

Dear Jesus:

Jesus with skin on:

"The cross is the key. If I lose this key I fumble. The universe will not open to me. But with the key in my hand I know I hold its secret."[4]
—E. Stanley Jones

Checking It Out

Rembrandt, the famous Dutch artist, painted a picture of the crucifixion. The center of the picture, of course, is Jesus on the cross. Then you notice the crowd milling around the cross. As your eyes drift to the edge of the picture, you see another figure standing in the shadows. It is Rembrandt himself! He is helping to crucify Jesus! But more importantly, he is receiving the love and forgiveness that flowed from the cross.

Just like Rembrandt, we put Jesus on the cross. But the story doesn't end there. Incredibly, just as Rembrandt experienced, Jesus showed us the greatest example of His love and forgiveness. The apostle Paul said in Romans 5:8,

"But God demonstrates his own love for us in this: While we were still sinners, Christ died for us."

Hot Notes:

Getting the Point

Read the account of the crucifixion in Mark 15:16-41.

The Roman judge read the same ritual for crucifixion every time: "The sentence is that this man should be taken to the cross." Then he turned and said, "Go, soldier, and prepare the cross."

Mob Mockery

In preparation for the cross, the soldiers took Jesus to the palace, called the Praetorium. Jesus was led across the walkway back into the barracks where the soldiers lived. In a large room Jesus found Himself surrounded by a battalion of some 600 Roman soldiers living in the barracks. The scene was not a pretty one.

The soldiers stripped Jesus naked, His body a swollen mass of bruised and battered flesh. They decided that since He was a king He needed a scepter, a robe and a crown. For a scepter they used a sticklike reed taken from a nearby plant. One of the soldiers threw in a cast-off rag for a robe. His crown consisted of thorns, some measuring 3½ inches in length.

Sarcastically they hailed Him as "King of the Jews." One by one they approached Him, knelt down before Him and pretended to worship Him. Then they stood up and spit on Jesus. They took the stick out of His hand and beat Him on the head with it. They dug the crown of thorns deep into His head. His face was covered with spit and blood. They stripped the purple robe from His back. The blood had already had time to clot. When they ripped it off, it took the scabs off with it. Then they led Him out to crucify Him.

Cruel Crucifixion

Several aspects of that gruesome experience help us grasp a tiny bit of the pain Jesus endured for us (Mark 15:21-32):

• The walk to the cross

Once the cross was prepared, then the victim carried it from the place of the sentence to the place of crucifixion. Placed in the hollow square of four Roman soldiers, the victim struggled to drag the heavy crossbeam. The soldiers in front carried the sign that indicated the crime. They took the longest route in order to make a spectacle of the victim. At the death site the crossbeam was attached to a vertical beam already in place. Physically Jesus' body was in shock. Along the way, He collapsed. The soldiers forced Simon of Cyrene, a black man, to carry the cross. Jesus was so weak they "brought him" (v. 22) to the cross.

• The nailing to the cross

The cross was laid on the ground and nailed together. Before they hammered the nails in, the soldiers offered Him a drink to kill the pain, but He did not take it. They stripped Jesus of His clothing and stretched Him out on the cross. His hands were nailed first. The soldiers found the spot on each wrist where the two bones came together near the pulse. The soldiers then drove the iron spikes through the wrist and into the wood. The feet were more difficult. The knees had to be bent; if not, the victim would not be able to push up and get air, therefore suffocating to death immediately. The soldiers then pounded the long spike through both feet. Between the prisoners' legs was a wedge of wood which took the weight of the cross when raised upright. Otherwise the nails would tear the flesh and bones and the victim would come loose from the cross. Then the criminal was raised upright and the cross dropped about two feet into a hole. The jolt of the cross falling into the hole intensified the pain.

• The torture on the cross

From this point on, the victim fought for his life. The awkward position exerted tremendous weight on the arms and shoulders. After a few minutes, the body ached horribly. The nerves were shattered and the wounds began to swell. In time, infection set in. Ultimately the victim experienced death by suffocation. Raising and dropping his body to catch his breath, he would become desperate. The thirst, the pain and the insects gradually weakened his body. When he could fight no longer, the victim died, unable to draw another breath. A victim could hang on for days, but Jesus died in six hours.

• The elements around the cross

In customary fashion the executioners took the crucified man's clothes. They decided who got what by throwing dice. With Jesus they had five articles of clothing to divide—the inner robe, outer robe, sandals, girdle and head covering. Each one took one of the articles, which left the expensive outer robe. That is what they threw dice for. The inscription over the cross was what Pilate used to get back at the Jews for what they had done. The inscription read, "This is Jesus of Nazareth, the king of the Jews." The Jews got furious because they said He only "claimed to be king of the Jews" but Pilate refused to change it. Then Jesus was crucified between two thieves. This placed Him on the lowest rung of the social order. Even in that, God was working His will as the prophecy from Isaiah 53:12, "... *[He] was numbered with the transgressors,"* was fulfilled.

• The verbal abuse at the cross

It would seem that at this point people would show some mercy and leave Jesus alone. But not so. Those passing by stopped to hurl insults. They must have heard these accusations from the religious leaders, since they had said the same things earlier. They yelled, *"So! You who are going to destroy the temple and build it in three days, come down from the cross and save yourself!"* (Mark 15:29, 30).

They viewed Him as a phony Messiah.

Then they were joined by the chief priests and scribes. Venom continued to spew out of their mouths as a result of their total hatred of Jesus. You would think these religious leaders would have some restraint. Yet they snarled at Him, *"He saved others . . . but he can't save himself! Let this Christ, this King of Israel, come down now from the cross, that we may see and believe"* (Mark 15:31, 32).

The robbers on the cross even hurled abuse at Him. But we know that one changed his mind and turned to Jesus on the cross (Luke 23:39-43). The heart of their accusations was that Jesus did not come down from the cross. Precisely! It is because He stayed there that we believe in Him!

Utter Abandonment

At high noon ("the sixth hour") darkness came over the whole earth for three hours. In the heat of the day, there came a supernatural darkness! The Father had expressed Himself through nature (Mark 15:33). The most painful moment had arrived. Jesus had never known even the slightest separation from His Father. He called to His Father, *"My God, my God, why have you forsaken me?"* (Mark 15:34) and for the first time in all of eternity His Father did not answer.

Jesus experienced the separation that sin brings. He literally experienced Hell. The Sinless One identified with man's sin and took it on Himself. Right then He took on the sin and guilt of the world. He experienced separation from His Father so that we would no longer have to.

Then Jesus breathed His last. In an awesome visible act of the removal of sin from our lives, the temple curtain ripped—from top to bottom. Unbelievable! This elaborately woven veil measured six feet thick. God tore it from top to bottom to symbolize that there is now no separation between God and man (Mark 15:38)!

Heavy Thoughts:

Looking Inside

Jesus passed from life to death, so that we can pass from death to life!

"He himself bore our sins in his body on the tree, so that we might die to sins and live for righteousness; by his wounds you have been healed" (1 Peter 2:24).

Dear Jesus:

Jesus with skin on:

The Great Equalizer

"Death stung himself to death when he stung Christ."[5]
—*William Romaine*

Ⓒhecking It Out

Here's a riddle for you: "One dead for every person."

Think about it. What does that mean? Death comes to everyone. It is the great equalizer. The closest I have been to death was sitting by my dad until he drew his last breath. Suddenly it hit me—he won't speak again, smile again, laugh again. But when I got perspective I realized, he's not here—he's there! He is speaking and smiling and laughing. And one day I'll see him again, because I'll be there too.

Jesus died. Even He was not spared. And they put Him in the tomb. But He did not stay there long! "Where, O death, is your victory? Where, O death is your sting?" (1 Corinthians 15:55).

Hot Notes:

Ⓖetting the Point

Read Luke 23:50-56.

Through the years people have tried to discredit Jesus on two counts: He did not die and He was not raised from the dead. Yet we have an account of Jesus' burial. He did die just like everyone else who has died. He not only died, but His body decayed to the point that He went to *"the dust of death"* (Psalm 22:15). Yet His Father arranged the circumstances in such a way that the body of His Son would be protected and then prepared for the great Resurrection Day!

Protecting Jesus' Body from Destruction

At three o'clock Jesus was dead. How would they get His body off the cross? The Romans often left bodies on the cross for days to make an example out of those who did not obey Roman law. If no one claimed the body then, in due time, the soldiers would throw it into the city dump to let the dogs and vultures dispose of it. Jesus' Father certainly did not want the body of His Son desecrated in a garbage dump.

At 6:00 P.M. the Jewish Sabbath began. After that no work could be done, so they would have to leave the body on the cross. Late in the afternoon, between three and six o'clock, Joseph of Arimathea stepped on the scene. God protected Jesus' body through Joseph's courage.

Who was Joseph? He was a rich man from the city of Arimathea. He sat with the Sanhedrin, one of seventy people who ruled Israel and had sentenced Jesus to death. He lived as *"a good and upright man"* (Luke 23:50). He had strong character and an unblemished reputation. He was a devout Jew who believed the Old Testament prophecies about the Messiah. He was *"waiting for the kingdom of God"* (v. 51). Most importantly, he was a follower of Jesus. We see Joseph's courage in two acts toward Jesus:

• Before the Sanhedrin

They tried Jesus and sent Him to the cross. But Joseph protested—he *"had not consented to their decision and action"* (v. 51). Joseph had come to believe that Jesus was the true Messiah. Before the crucifixion he kept his beliefs to himself. He was fearful of what the other members would say. But when Jesus came before the Sanhedrin the night before, Joseph took his stand.

• Before Pilate

Joseph knew Pilate had hostility toward the Jews. He had witnessed Pilate's anger earlier in the day when the Jewish leaders led the crowd to choose Barabbas. The chances of Pilate giving him the body were slim to none. But he went anyway (v. 52).

According to Mark's account, Pilate had concerns about whether or not Jesus was dead. Crucifixion victims often survived for days. Pilate sent for the centurion to verify it and the centurion said it was so. They had thrust a spear in Jesus' side; water and blood had come out—a sign of death.

Preparing Jesus' Body for the Resurrection

Having completed His suffering on the cross, the Father made certain that Jesus' body received the treatment that it deserved. Joseph stepped up again to prepare Jesus' body for burial.

• Taking down the body (v. 53)

Back at Golgotha, Nicodemus, a few servants, some Roman soldiers and Joseph took the body off the cross. Joseph hurried to get the body down for two reasons. First, the Jews had strict rules about a body left hanging on the cross overnight. In his book *The Resurrection Factor*, Josh McDowell said, "If he is left [hanging] overnight, a negative command is thereby transgressed. For it is written, his body shall not remain all night upon the tree, but you shall bury him the same day, for he is hanged because of a curse against God."

Secondly, the Sabbath began at 6 P.M. That time was approaching rapidly. When they got the body down from the cross, they transported it immediately to the place where they would bury it. In Jesus' case, they took the body to a private tomb owned by Joseph, close to Golgotha.

• Wrapping up the body (vv. 53-56)

According to the Jewish burial custom, the Jews would place the body on a stone table in the burial chamber. Then they would wash it with warm water. Next, they used various aromatic spices to embalm the body. For Jesus they used about 75 pounds of spices. When Herod died, it required 500 servants to carry the spices! In addition they used aloes, a dust from a fragrant wood, and myrrh, a gummy substance.

After all the body members were straightened, the corpse was clothed in graveclothes made of white, expensive linens. Starting at the feet, they would wrap the body with a clean linen cloth, cut in strips. Between the folds they placed myrrh and aloes. They would wrap to the armpits, put the arms down and wrap them, then finish with the neck. A separate piece was wrapped around the head. The body weighed 115 to 120 pounds more than normal. In the fourth century, John Chrysostom stated, "the myrrh used was a drug which adheres so closely to the body that the graveclothes could not easily be removed."

• Laying in the body (v. 53)

The tomb where they laid the body of Jesus actually had been purchased by Joseph of Arimathea for his own burial. He gave it to Jesus. The tombs were located in a garden close to Golgotha. These cave-like tombs belonged only to the rich. They were cut out of the rock on the side of the hill. Often they had two compartments: an outer chamber where a person entered and a smaller inner chamber where the body was placed on a slab cut out of the rock. This was where they laid the body of Jesus.

• Sealing over the body (v. 54)

Joseph and the crew, working on getting Jesus' body prepared, were in a hurry. Time was running out until the Sabbath began at 6 o'clock. To keep the body protected, they pushed the stone over the front of the tomb. It was such a large stone that it weighed between one and a half to two tons. It would take about twenty men to move it. So how did this small crew get it into place? The stone was elevated at a slight angle above the tomb. It was held in place by a wedge of wood or stone. When the wedge was removed, gravity did its work. The stone rolled down a groove and crashed in front of the tomb.

• Looking at the location of the body (v. 55)

Two women watched the entire procedure. Mary Magdalene and Mary, the mother of Joses, sat across from the gravesite. Later, questions were raised about what happened to Jesus' body. But from this one verse we understand that there should have been no confusion about that. These women saw the location of the tomb and they watched the body being laid in it. They were eyewitnesses. That was important because in New Testament times two witnesses were needed to establish the truth of any event. Both of these women had firsthand knowledge of the facts concerning Jesus' burial.

Heavy Thoughts:

Looking Inside

When Jesus died on Friday, God prepared Him for the resurrection on Sunday. God took Joseph of Arimathea through the same "dying and rising" process. Joseph took great risk to secure Jesus' body. He had to die to himself—to his past life with his Sanhedrin friends who were enemies of Christ. Then he had to live his new life by identifying with Jesus on the cross. When he did that, God used him to set the stage for the greatest event in all of human history—the resurrection of Jesus!

God wants to take you through the same "dying and rising" process. The apostle Paul proclaims, **"Our old sinful selves were crucified with Christ so that sin might lose its power in our lives. We are no longer slaves to sin. For when we died with Christ we were set free from the power of sin. And since we died with Christ, we know we will also share his new life" (Romans 6:6, 7, NLT).**

Dear Jesus:

Jesus with skin on:

Body Functions

" . . . the only ultimate way to conquer evil is to let it be smothered within a willing, living human being. When it is absorbed there like blood in a sponge or a spear into one's heart, it loses its power and goes no further."[6]
—M. Scott Peck

Checking It Out

Harry weighed over 300 pounds. His body was so out of control that he could not get through the door of his prison cell. His body and soul were wasting away. Then he met Christ. He made a choice that while getting his soul in shape, he would do something about his body too. His motto became "Fat must scat!" He started with one push-up. That's all he could do, and that about killed him. But he stayed with it. When I met him he weighed 185 pounds and could run for miles!

Like Harry, we need to get our bodies in good condition and then keep them that way. But Jesus did it the opposite way. As a carpenter He always kept His body in good condition, but at one point He allowed it to be crushed for us!

"He himself bore our sins in his body on the tree, so that we might die to sins and live for righteousness; by his wounds you have been healed" (1 Peter 2:24).

Hot Notes:

Getting the Point

When we eat the communion bread and drink the wine, we celebrate the broken body and shed blood of Jesus. That serves as a vivid symbol and a powerful illustration of what Jesus did for us on the cross.

We have taken a look at what happened at the cross, but now let's see what that means. When we take communion and say, "This is the body of Jesus broken for you," what do we mean by that?

The body functions as a pretty amazing machine. For example:
- We take an average of 20 breaths per minute. Over 70 years that is 36,691,200 breaths.
- We have five million red blood cells per cubic inch throughout our bodies.
- Both of our eyes have 107,000,000 cells in them.
- Each person has 100,000 hairs on his or her head (give or take a few thousand!).
- It takes 70 muscles just to flex the little finger.

The Greek dramatist Sophocles said, "Numberless are the world's wonders, but none—none more wondrous than the body of a man."

But the body can be thrown out of its delicate balance very easily. Cancer can make it diseased. Getting hit by a car can cause it severe pain. Having a bone in a cast causes its muscles to atrophy. If it gets cut, it bleeds. We avoid those things at all possible cost.

When we look at Jesus and realize that He pursued having His body broken, we should stand in awe!

Disease Embraced

The human body hates disease. It is built to fight it.

In the book *In His Image*, Paul Brand says, "Battle imagery is particularly appropriate to describe what happens inside our bodies, for with an array of menacing weapons and defenders, our bodies declare war on the invaders. At the first sign of an invasion, a chemical Paul Revere alarm sounds, and numerous body systems hasten into action. Capillaries dilate, like inflatable tunnels, to allow a swarm of armed defenders into the combat zone. White blood cells of five distinct types form the initial assault forces. Transparent, bristling with weapons and possessing a Houdini-like ability to slip between other cells, the white cells are the body's chief fighters. During healthy periods, 25 billion white cells circulate freely throughout the blood and 25 billion more loiter on blood vessel walls."[7]

Jesus' body hated the disease of sin. But instead of fighting it off, He embraced it. He took the disease on Himself so we could overcome it.

God does not tolerate sin. His personality won't allow it. One aspect of His character is that He is holy. Because of His holiness, sin is not allowed where He is. Since it contaminates every person, no one is allowed in His presence. That's what Paul is talking about in Romans 3:23 when he says, *"For all have sinned and fall short of the glory of God."*

He condemns sin in us and demands that we pay for it. That payment is death. God has given us the death penalty. Romans 6:23 says, *"For the wages of sin is death. . . ."* However, instead of us dying of the disease of sin, God loved us so much that He sent His Son Jesus to embrace the disease and get rid of it. He gave us *". . . the gift of God is eternal life in Christ Jesus our Lord"* (Romans 6:23).

When John the Baptist saw Jesus, he said, *"Look, the Lamb of God, who takes away the sin of the world!"* (John 1:29). At the cross we saw how great the price was that Jesus paid. God sent darkness over the land from 12 o'clock until 3 o'clock so no one could see the agony of Jesus. *All* of the accumulated sins of *all* of the people throughout *all* of history were embraced by Him at that time. Those sins separated Him from His Father for the first time since eternity began.

Hurt with Pain

The human body is designed to feel pain. Because of a marvelous and complex nervous system that is extremely sensitive, we experience pain. If we did not know pain, we would harm ourselves.

People who get leprosy lose their fingers and toes. Those appendages become stubs. Eventually they lose their ability to feel pain. So the danger is not the leprosy itself, but the inability to feel pain. That leads to severe burns that the lepers don't even know they have. Or it can cause horrible blisters from constant rubbing on a foot that doesn't feel. Absence of pain is a horrible thing!

But Jesus came to feel our pain. God told Adam that his sin brought a curse and the curse brought pain (Genesis 3:17). Deuteronomy 21:23 says that *"anyone who is hung on a tree is under God's curse."* Because Jesus chose to identify with our sin, He was under a curse. That curse resulted in pain.

When they nailed His hands and feet with the spikes, dropped the cross into the socket with a sickening thud—ripping flesh, causing His bones to go out of socket, and impairing His breathing, we get a small glimpse of how horrible His pain was. When they pierced His side and the blood and water flowed out, not only was that a sign of death, but also of dying from a broken heart. The physical pain was nothing compared to the unimaginable spiritual pain He endured for our sins.

Jesus' body experienced deep pain. He volunteered to endure that pain because of His even deeper love for us. That's what it means when someone serving communion to you says, "This is the body of Jesus broken for you."

Wounds Healed

The human body has an amazing capacity for healing itself. When you fall and cut your knee, immediately blood and lymph cells flow to the injury to clean it. The blood clots and the wound begins to heal.

Jesus' body brings healing to our wounds. First Peter 2:24 makes that very clear: *"by his wounds you have been healed."* Peter understood this from reading Isaiah 53:5: *"But he was pierced for our transgressions, he was crushed for our iniquities; the punishment that brought us peace was upon him, and by his wounds we are healed."* The stripes from His scourging, the holes in His hands, feet and side—all of these were Jesus' wounds.

This is a strange approach: the physician willingly suffered so His sufferers could be healed. That is why Jesus is called the "Wounded Healer." He is the only person in all of history who can call Himself that. Of all the other gods who claim deity, none ever suffered and died for his subjects. But Jesus was hurt so we could receive healing!

Heavy Thoughts:

Looking Inside

Jesus took our disease, our pain and our wounds that came from sin. He allowed His body to be broken for us. Not only does that call for the deepest sense of gratitude for what He did, but it only makes sense to let the Wounded Healer heal us.

Ask yourself:

What disease of sin does He need to get rid of in my life?

What hurts do you have that are caused by the pain of your sin or someone else's?

What wounds need healing?

"The Lord Jesus, on the night he was betrayed, took bread, and when he had given thanks, he broke it and said, 'This is my body, which is for you; do this in remembrance of me'" **(1 Corinthians 11:23, 24).**

Dear Jesus:

Jesus with skin on:

Life Blood

"One drop of Christ's blood is worth more than heaven and earth."[8]
—Martin Luther

Checking It Out

Has anyone ever taken your blood pressure? Ask your doctor to try this experiment next time. Wrap the cuff around your arm. Pump it up to 200 mm of mercury. Then make a fist ten times in succession. Release it, then do it again. You will scream with pain. Why? Because the blood supply from your heart is cut off to your arm. The muscle action produces waste that needs to be flushed out. As a result of no blood—pain! And if you would keep doing it, the loss of blood would cause you to lose the life in your arm and you would need to have it amputated. So take the cuff off now!

Blood is absolutely necessary for the proper function of that arm. Without it, the arm will die. In the same way, the blood of Jesus shed on the cross gives life to us spiritually. Without it, we die!

"For you know that it was not with perishable things such as silver or gold that you were redeemed from the empty way of life handed down to you from your forefathers, but with the precious blood of Christ, a lamb without blemish or defect" (1 Peter 1:18, 19).

Hot Notes:

Getting the Point

Since my son Scott is studying to become a doctor, we have had numerous conversations about blood. When the subject comes up, people say things like "yuck." They see blood as repulsive. But the apostle Peter described it as "precious."

Why is human blood precious? Our bodies contain five to seven quarts of it made up of plasma, corpuscles and platelets. Every cubic millimeter (a speck the size of a pinhead) contains 5,000,000 living cells. Those cells last 110 to 120 days. To replenish the dead ones, the body manufactures 2,000,000 new cells every second.

Here's how it works: "60,000 miles of blood vessels link every living cell. . . . Highways narrow down to one-lane roads, then bike paths, then footpaths, until finally the diameter of a human hair. In such narrow confines the cells are stripped of food and oxygen and loaded down with carbon dioxide and urea. . . . The red cells, like bloated bags of jelly and iron, drift along in a river until they reach the smallest capillary, where gases fizz and wheeze in and out of surface membranes. From there the red cells rush to the kidney for a thorough scrubbing, then back to the lungs for a refill. And the journey begins again.

"The . . . journey, even to the extremity of the big toe, lasts a mere twenty seconds. An average red cell endured the cycle of loading, unloading, and jostling through the body for a half million round trips over four months. In one final journey, to the spleen, the embattered cell is stripped bare by scavenger cells and recycled into new cells. 300 billion such red cells die and are replaced every day."[9]

Amazing! With our human blood that precious, why is Jesus' blood even more precious?

Blood Saves Lives

According to the American Red Cross, "Blood is the nation's #1 medicine in the saving of lives." The blood of Christ is a transfusion that saves us. All of us have a diseased heart that produces "bad blood." That has been passed down to us from generation to generation. We were born with *"the empty way of life handed down to you from your forefathers"* (1 Peter 1:18).

Jesus shed His blood on the cross to "redeem us"—to give us another chance. He replaces our old heart with a new one. God promises, *"I will give them an undivided heart and put a new spirit in them; I will remove from them their heart of stone and give them a heart of flesh"* (Ezekiel 11:19).

Blood Cleanses

When blood gets on a white shirt, it doesn't look very clean. In fact, it stains it and makes it dirty. So how can we say blood cleanses? Look inside the body.

Close to every blood cell is a blood capillary. The red blood cells pump oxygen in and absorb waste products. Then the red blood cells deliver that hazardous waste to organs that can dump them outside the body through the lungs and kidney. Just like blood cleanses the harmful waste out of our bodies, the blood of Jesus cleans out the lethal waste of sin that keeps us from having a healthy relationship with God. That cleansing comes through a lamb without blemish or spot (1 Peter 1:19).

Israel's greatest day was Passover. It began when Moses instructed the people of Israel to place blood over each door so that the angel of death would pass over that home. That blood was from a lamb that was perfect—no blemishes. The homes with the blood over the door were cleansed from sin and escaped death. The ones that did not have the blood over the door were not clean and were not protected from death. The blood of the lamb made the difference.

Since then, the Jewish people have celebrated Yom Kippur, the "Day of Atonement"—the most significant of Jewish celebrations. They killed a bull and sprinkled its blood to atone for the sins of the priest. Next they sacrificed a male goat for the sins of the people. The priest sprinkled the blood in the Holy of Holies inside the temple. After that, they took a second goat, which they called a "scapegoat," confessed their sins, and placed them on the goat. Then they drove him out into the desert where he carried away the sins of the people.

The "Day of Atonement" reminded people that their sacrifices were not adequate to take away their own sin. Their sacrifices were only temporary. That's why they did this every year. They waited for a perfect lamb—a sinless, spotless lamb—to permanently take away their sins. Jesus was that Lamb.

Hebrews 9:26 says, *"But now he has appeared once for all at the end of the ages to do away with sin by the sacrifice of himself."* The blood of Jesus Christ, shed on the cross, takes away the sin of the world and our sin, and makes us able to stand clean, pure and holy before God. Awesome!

Blood Gives Life

"For lack of a donor a life was lost," the radio announcer exclaimed. He continued, "I'm not talking about money, I'm talking about blood. When a certain type of blood is needed for a certain person in a certain place at a certain time, a million dollars is useless . . . blood is the only answer!"

There is no substitute for blood! When blood is needed, nothing else will suffice. It's either blood or death. When we think about blood, we think of gruesome cuts, stitches and emergency rooms. But in the medical profession blood symbolizes life, not death. It feeds every cell in the body with precious nutrients that cause our bodies to stay healthy and function properly.

Even when we think of the blood of Christ, we associate it with His death. But He shed His blood that brought death to Him, so we could have life. His blood gives life. In one of His most radical statements, Jesus made this point clear: *"Jesus said to them, 'I tell you the truth, unless you eat the flesh of the Son of Man and drink his blood, you have no life in you. Whoever eats my flesh and drinks my blood has eternal life, and I will raise him up at the last day. For my flesh is real food and my blood is real drink. Whoever eats my flesh and drinks my blood remains in me, and I in him. Just as the living Father sent me and I live because of the Father, so the one who feeds on me will live because of me"* (John 6:53-57).

To a Jew who never ate meat with blood in it, what Jesus said sounded like fingernails scratching across a blackboard. Jews never ingested blood; they always poured it out. But Jesus said, "Drink my blood." The thought of that seemed revolting. Why was He so offensive?

Jesus wanted to make a radical point: take My life inside of you, so our lives become totally intertwined—intimate and personal. Take in My life until you are totally saturated with Me. Fill your life up with Me.

When we go to the communion table and drink the cup, that not only symbolizes Jesus' death for us—His shed blood, but so much more. It symbolizes His present life. We cannot live without the continual transfusion that His lifeblood provides. Take it! Drink it! It gives life!

Heavy Thoughts:

Looking Inside

Jesus' blood saves us, cleanses us and gives us life. How valuable is that to you?

Are you ready to "drink His blood" in the sense of filling your life up with Him every day, just like you drink a big glass of water?

"In the same way, after supper he took the cup, saying, 'This cup is the new covenant in my blood; do this, whenever you drink it, in remembrance of me'" (1 Corinthians 11:25).

Dear Jesus:

Jesus with skin on:

Rip-Off or Reality?

chapter 5
Jesus no equal

Anyone can kill another person. But what about bringing someone back to life? Several world superpowers have weapons equal to 35 tons of TNT for every person in the world. But that's mickey mouse stuff compared to the power it would take to bring someone back from the dead.

Jesus claimed access to that kind of power. He told His disciples, "Listen, we are going down to Jerusalem. I will suffer and die there, but keep cool because three days later I will rise again" (Matthew 16:21-26; Mark 8:31-37; 9:9; Luke 9:18-25, *author's paraphrase*). He made it plain that everything He said and did would hinge on the resurrection.

Jesus' bodily resurrection from the dead is absolutely critical to the validity of Christianity. The apostle Paul said, *"And if Christ has not been raised, our preaching is useless and so is your faith"* (1 Corinthians 15:14). Jesus' resurrection establishes His uniqueness. No other religious leader has ever claimed to rise from the dead. If we could visit the graves of Buddha, Muhammad, Confucius or numerous others who started religious movements, we would find their skeletal remains. But at the tomb of Jesus, all we find is an empty grave.

Of equal importance is the fact that if Jesus' resurrection is reality, then He has the right and the power to change your life and mine. Jesus said, *"I am the resurrection and the life. He who believes in me will live, even though he dies; and whoever lives and believes in me will never die"* (John 11:25, 26).

Did Jesus Christ really rise from the dead? The evidence says yes! That doesn't mean that the validity of Christianity can be "proven" like the latest scientific theory. God cannot be crammed into a test tube. However, faith in Jesus Christ and in the reality of His resurrection does not have to be "blind" faith either. The historical evidence stacks up solidly on the side of the belief that Jesus was literally raised from the dead.

The Witness of the Scholars

Some people believe that all educated persons consider the resurrection a myth. The fact is that many great thinkers have defended the truth of Jesus' being raised from the dead. In fact, for 429 years after Jesus lived, no one wrote a single word disputing the reality of the resurrection.[1]

Professor Thomas Arnold, once chairman of Modern History at Oxford University, said, "I have been used for many years to studying the histories of other times, and to examine and weigh the evidence of those who have written about them, and I know of no one fact in the history of mankind which is proved by better and fuller evidence of every sort, to the understanding of a fair inquirer, than the great sign which God has given us that Christ died and rose again from the dead."[2]

Lord Lyndhurst, one of the greatest legal authorities in English history, wrote, "I know pretty well what evidence is; and I tell you such evidence as that for the resurrection has never broken down yet."[3]

Simon Greenleaf was a great professor of law at Harvard. His books are still studied in law schools today. Two students challenged Greenleaf concerning whether or not the resurrection would stand in a court of law. He took the challenge and said, "The resurrection of Jesus Christ is the most established fact of history."[4]

Frank Morison, journalist, engineer, rationalist, thought Jesus' life had been a good example for the world, but he could not buy the "resurrection myth." He set out to disprove it, and finished his research a believer.[5]

Lord Lyttleton and Gilbert Benjamin West were professors at Oxford University. They took a six-month study leave and set out to disprove the resurrection of Jesus Christ and the conversion of Paul. Concluding their research, they both admitted that the resurrection and Paul's conversion could be substantiated from a scholar's standpoint. They then gave their lives to Jesus Christ. On the flyleaf of the book they coauthored as a result of their study, they wrote, "Blame not before thou hast examined the truth." In other words, don't reject until you have examined the evidence.[6]

Josh McDowell, speaker and author, faced up to the resurrection issue during his college days. Several of his Christian friends challenged McDowell, who was not a Christian, to intellectually examine the claims of Christ. After studying the evidence, he came to the conclusion that he would have been "intellectually dishonest" with himself if he did not believe.[7] He now travels worldwide sharing his insights on the validity of Jesus Christ as the Son of God.

McDowell has this to say about the resurrection: "A believer in Jesus Christ today can have complete confidence, as did the first Christians, that his faith is based not on myth or legend, but on the solid historical fact of the risen Christ and the empty tomb."[8]

From an historical viewpoint, educators, lawyers, and scientists alike have confirmed the validity of the resurrection. The witness of a vast number of scholars indicates that Jesus is alive. But that's only the beginning.

Let's check out some of the facts of the actual resurrection event.

The Undisturbed Graveclothes

"Early on the first day of the week, while it was still dark, Mary Magdalene went to the tomb and saw that the stone had been removed from the entrance. So she came running to Simon Peter and the other disciple, the one Jesus loved, and said, 'They have taken the Lord out of the tomb, and we don't know where they have put him!'

"So Peter and the other disciple started for the tomb. Both were running, but the other disciple outran Peter and reached the tomb first. He bent over and looked in at the strips of linen lying there but did not go in. Then Simon Peter, who was behind him, arrived and went into the tomb. He saw the strips of linen lying there, as well as the burial cloth that had been around Jesus' head. The cloth was folded up by itself, separate from the linen. Finally the other disciple, who had reached the tomb first, also went inside. He saw and believed" (John 20:1-8).

What did they see? Whatever it was must have been significant because these few Bible verses mention three times that Peter and John "saw." The word used for "saw" means "to see and understand." They saw the wrapping with no body in it. They saw the burial cloth that had been wound around Jesus' head "folded up by itself." With this evidence in front of them, they saw and believed.

The Empty Tomb

Matthew 27:57-66 records the many precautions that were taken in the burial of Jesus' body. The Jewish authorities were afraid Jesus' disciples would steal the body, then claim that He was alive. They took several steps which, along with some of the normal burial procedures, would make sure that Jesus stayed in the tomb—or so they thought.

First, they put Him in a "new tomb" (v. 60) carved out of solid rock. Inside were several stone slabs recessed into the walls of the cave. Eventually a body was to be placed on each slab.

Second, Jesus' body was wrapped in a "clean linen cloth" (v. 59). The body was brought in and laid on one of the stone slabs. According to the Jewish burial custom, the people who buried Jesus also brought about 75 pounds of spices (John 19:39, 40).

With yards of linen cloth, they wrapped the body, placing the spices and a gummy substance on the wrapping. They wrapped the cloth around the legs, then around the trunk up to the neck. Then the spices and gummy substance hardened. Jesus probably weighed about 115-120 pounds heavier than His normal body weight. He was a mummy! Imagine how hard it would have been to get out of those wrappings.

Third, a big stone was rolled against the door. We don't know just how much the stone weighed, but some authorities speculate it was as much as two tons. Almost all agree it would have taken at least three or four men to move it once the stone was placed in the tomb entrance.

Fourth, the tomb was made *"secure by putting a seal on the stone"* (v. 66). Cords were stretched and fastened across the stone. The Roman emperor's official insignia was inscribed in clay or wax on the outside of the tomb. If anyone broke the seal, it meant death. Jesus wasn't supposed to get out!

Fifth, the Romans placed a guard (v. 65) around the tomb. Josh McDowell observes that many people picture the "guard" as two skinny guys holding wooden spears and wearing miniskirts. But the real picture is of a 16-man security unit with each man responsible for six square feet of territory! These were Roman soldiers—the best in the world. Their methods are still used by the military today.

What Really Happened?

So what happened? There are a bunch of theories:

• The first view is that the Roman and Jewish leaders took the body.

Why would these leaders who had killed Jesus want His body out? They wouldn't. They wanted to protect their careers and they knew that if Jesus' body were missing, all of Palestine would be in an uproar. They wanted to keep the body in the tomb.

In addition, they certainly would have come up with the body after the disciples started telling everyone that Jesus was alive. In an effort to destroy Christianity, these Roman and Jewish leaders beat the disciples, jailed them and told them not to say another word. All the authorities had to do was to produce the body and the uproar would have been over. But they couldn't produce it because they didn't have it.

• A second view is that the disciples stole the body.

That's what the Roman and Jewish authorities wanted people to think (Matthew 28:11-15). But remember the guards, the 16 soldiers who were among the best in the world? If the guards allowed the emperor's seal to be broken, they would be brutally punished. One form of punishment called for a soldier's clothes to be taken off and placed at his feet. Then he was burned to death, his own clothes being used for fuel. No way were the guards going to let Jesus' body get away!

Now, remember the disciples? Did they steal the body? Eleven scruffy guys coming to take on the best soldiers in the world? You've got to be kidding! They couldn't even "toilet paper" someone's house without getting caught. The matchup would be like a seventh-grade football team taking on the Super Bowl champs.

Imagine the disciples sneaking up on the guards. They steal the soldiers' swords and wipe them out. They push away the huge stone. They steal the mummified body and tell everybody that Jesus is alive. It takes a pretty vivid imagination to believe that! The disciples could not have taken the body. First, they could never have overcome the Romans. Second, when persecuted and martyred for their faith in Christ, surely one of them would have admitted that the resurrection was a lie. Not one of them ever did.

• A third explanation of the resurrection is the "Swoon Theory."

In his book *The Passover Plot*, Hugh Schoenfeld theorizes that Jesus never died on the cross. He was merely thought to be dead. He was taken down from the cross and put into the tomb. The coolness of the tomb revived Him. He got out and showed Himself to His disciples, and claimed to be risen from the dead.

Imagine it! Jesus went through all of the suffering described in the last chapter. Blood mixed with water poured out of His side, providing medical evidence of His death. Several people handled His body and raised no questions about His being alive. Jesus was wrapped in mummifying substances and put in a cold, dark tomb with no food or water. So He revives, gets out of His mummified case, pushes away the huge stone, overcomes 16 of the world's best soldiers, walks to Jerusalem on nail-pierced feet and appears to His disciples as the picture of health. No way, José!

The best and most logical explanation is the biblical one—the tomb was empty because Jesus Christ was raised from the dead!

The Ten Appearances

The Bible tells us that Jesus appeared at least ten different times in 40 days after His resurrection. He was seen by as many as 500 people and by as few as one. He cooked. He ate fish. He talked. Some of His disciples even touched Him. Could all of these people who said they saw Him have had halluci-nations? For that many people on that many occasions to have had hallucinations would break all the laws of psychology. No—Jesus is alive!

The Disciples' Changed Lives

One of the greatest evidences for the resurrection is the changed lives of Jesus' disciples. Take Simon Peter for example. When Jesus was arrested, Peter let a young servant girl scare him into denying Christ (John 18:15-18). After Jesus' death, Peter and the other disciples hid out, afraid for their lives (John 20:19). But after witnessing Jesus' resurrection, the disciples appeared before the same court that only a few weeks before had condemned Jesus to death.

Peter courageously challenged the court by saying, *"It [the healing of a crippled man] is by the name of Jesus Christ of Nazareth, whom you crucified but whom God raised from the dead, that this man [the cripple] stands before you healed. . . . Salvation is found in no one else, for there is no other name under heaven given to men by which we must be saved"* (Acts 4:10, 12).

The court realized that Peter and John had changed. *"When they saw the courage of Peter and John and realized that they were unschooled, ordinary men, they were astonished and they took note that these men had been with Jesus"* (Acts 4:13).

Take the brother of Jesus, James, for another example. All along he had thought that Jesus was one brick shy of a full load. (See Mark 3:20, 21.) If your brother went around saying things like, "I am the door," "I am the vine" and "I am God," you would think he was weird too! Then, convinced of the real-ity of the resurrection, James recognized Jesus for who He really is. Listen to how he begins his book: *"James, a servant of God and of the Lord Jesus Christ"* (James 1:1).

Mark serves as another example of a changed life. The author of the second Gospel was a young teenager when Jesus taught the crowds in Galilee. His life was changed by the power of the resurrec-tion. Years later when he was an older man, he was asked to choose between denying Jesus' resur-rection or dying—he chose death. According to tradition, his killers tied a rope to each limb of his body, then tied a horse to each rope. Then they pulled his body apart. Mark knew the truth and he was willing to die for it.

Then there is Paul. How do we explain him? His passion was to persecute Christians. Radically changed by a resurrection encounter with Jesus, he proclaimed Jesus throughout the world at a great cost to himself. His number one goal in life was *"to know Christ and the power of his resurrection and the fellowship of sharing in his sufferings, becoming like him in his death"* (Philippians 3:10).

All of Jesus' disciples, except John, were killed for their faith in their Lord. People will lie to protect themselves. But people don't die for something they know to be a lie!

Personal Evidence

The miracle of changed lives is one piece of evidence that can be observed firsthand today. Hardened criminals become model citizens. Atheists become dedicated believers. Drug addicts are set free—and give Jesus the credit.

The changes in my own life have been less dramatic. But they are nonetheless a testimony to the power of the resurrected Jesus. In my teen years, I was selfish, cocky, overly ambitious, hungry for popularity and insensitive to people. Then the resurrection power of Jesus changed my life. One of the significant changes came in my family relationships.

One afternoon, when I was 16 and my sister Cathey was 13, I was working on a science poster. Cathey brought me something to drink, and when she offered me the glass, I ignored her. She stood there for a moment and when I still didn't take the glass, she poured it all over my poster. I jumped up and slapped her. She ran into the house and I ran after her. I was going to hit her again.

From that point on, our relationship drifted farther and farther apart. Even when I tried to do something nice for Cathey, it never seemed to work out. Later, she began to have some difficult circumstances in her life. In the middle of that period she told my mom, "You know, Barry has really been a crummy big brother to me." My mom told me what Cathey had said, and it broke my heart.

Since the science poster episode, I had received Jesus into my life, and my life had changed. I asked Him to show me how to have a good relationship with my sister. We talked and I confessed, "Cathey, I have been a crummy big brother to you." I listed all of the ways I had failed her. Then I asked, "Cathey, will you forgive me?" With tears in her eyes, she put her arms around me and said, "Barry, I love you and I forgive you." Immediately the barriers were gone—smashed by the resurrection power of Jesus Christ.

A Decision That Makes Sense

The resurrection of Jesus Christ is no rip-off. It's reality. So many people reject the truth without examining the evidence. Add to the evidence for the resurrection hundreds of fulfilled Bible prophecies, the impact of Jesus' life and teachings and His work in the world today—and believing in Jesus makes good sense.

Mentally accepting the evidence is not enough. Jesus is alive. Are you willing to let Him live in you? When you allow His resurrection power to control you, several things happen:

1. You have the life of Jesus in you.
"You, however, are controlled not by the sinful nature but by the Spirit, if the Spirit of God lives in you. And if anyone does not have the Spirit of Christ, he does not belong to Christ" (Romans 8:9).

2. You are a new person.
"Therefore, if anyone is in Christ, he is a new creation; the old has gone, the new has come!" (2 Corinthians 5:17).

3. You have all you need to live life at its best.

"Praise be to the God and Father of our Lord Jesus Christ, who has blessed us in the heavenly realms with every spiritual blessing in Christ" (Ephesians 1:3).

4. You no longer have to fear death.

"'Where, O death, is your victory? Where, O death, is your sting?' The sting of death is sin, and the power of sin is the law. But thanks be to God! He gives us the victory through our Lord Jesus Christ" (1 Corinthians 15:55-57).

5. You will live with God forever.

"I write these things to you who believe in the name of the Son of God so that you may know that you have eternal life" (1 John 5:13).

If you already have eternal life through Jesus living in your heart, you have access to His resurrection power. Pray for that power to control you so you can live for Christ, to change you so you can reflect Christ and to empower you so you can make a difference in the lives of people every day.

If you do not yet have eternal life through Jesus living in your heart, discuss your desire with the spiritual leaders at your church. By following Christ you can live forever!

Up Close and Personal

1. Why is it important to know whether or not Jesus was raised from the dead? (Add your own ideas to those in this chapter.) What difference would it make if He did not rise?

2. Review some of the evidence for the resurrection: the witness of scholars, the empty tomb and the precautions taken to keep Jesus' body in the grave, the ten appearances and the disciples' changed lives. Which do you personally find most convincing for you? Which do you think your friends will find intriguing?

3. Who do you know who can give personal evidence of a life changed by Jesus' resurrection power?

4. How have you experienced Christ's resurrection power in your own life?

5. What specific changes occur when you allow Jesus' resurrection power to control you? (Look at "A Decision That Makes Sense" on page 116 to refresh your memory.) Have you received that power by asking Jesus into your life? Are you letting Him control, change and empower you every day?

The Resurrection of Jesus

day 1 — Beyond "E.T."

"If all of the evidence is weighed carefully and fairly, it is indeed justifiable, according to the canons of historical research, to conclude that the tomb in which Jesus was buried was actually empty on the morning of the first Easter. And no shred of evidence has yet been discovered in literary sources, epigraphy, or archeology that would disprove this statement."[9]
—Paul Maier

Checking It Out

Several years ago the movie *E.T.* was a box office hit. That little alien touched our hearts when he croaked: "E.T., phone home." He almost died, but communication was made with his spaceship. At that point the wilted flowers in the room came alive. His human friends sneaked him out of the hospital. The big chase began to get to the spaceship so he would not die. Bikes flew across the sky, eluding the police. After making contact with the spaceship, Elliott said good-bye to E.T. He took his flowers and went home.

Amazingly our culture buys into an incredibly fictional story like *E.T.* but absolutely refuses to concede the reality of the resurrection of Jesus Christ! Check any secular high school or university textbook and the writers handle the resurrection of Jesus in one of two ways:

- **Silence.** They say Jesus was an historical figure who died by crucifixion, then they skip the resurrection to discuss how the church grew. This leaves the reader puzzled about all the fuss over Jesus of Nazareth.
- **Doubt.** They qualify the report saying, "Jesus rose from the dead on Easter morning, so His disciples believed." They fail to look at the resurrection of Jesus objectively and historically.

The resurrection is the crux of history. If it did not happen, our faith is worthless. If it did, then Jesus is alive today with the ability to invade and change our lives by His resurrection power.

"'Don't be alarmed,' [the angel] said. 'You are looking for Jesus the Nazarene, who was crucified. He has risen! He is not here. See the place where they laid him'" (Mark 16:6).

Hot Notes:

Getting the Point

Read the account of the resurrection in Mark 16:1-8.

For the resurrection to make sense, we must look at it and then embrace it in three areas: our intellect, emotions and will.

Our Intellect

Can we believe the resurrection with intellectual honesty? That is the question. Many proofs exist that the resurrection is credible. (See the information at the beginning of this chapter.) From Mark 16:1-8, let's look at five proofs of the resurrection:

1. The Appearance to the Women

Mark states that when the Sabbath had ended, *"Mary Magdalene, Mary the mother of James, and Salome bought spices so that they might go to anoint Jesus' body. Very early on the first day of the week, just after sunrise, they were on their way to the tomb"* (Mark 16:1, 2).

When we take into account all four Gospels, half a dozen or more women came to the tomb. That the women are the first to discover the resurrection, rather than Jesus' male disciples, establishes the reality of the resurrection. In that culture women were seen as inferior and were not credible witnesses. Therefore, if the resurrection accounts had been made up by the disciples, they would not have made it up like this—with the women in the lead, especially as eyewitnesses.

2. The Preparation of the Body

The Sabbath ended at 6 P.M. Saturday. After that, the women purchased the burial spices. Then the next morning, Sunday, as the sun came up, they came to the tomb. They did not come to embalm the body, because that had already been done by Joseph (John 19:38-42). But they came to sprinkle the body with fragrant oils and spices as an act of respect.

We know that Jesus' body had already been confirmed as dead by Pilate and then was buried according to the Jewish burial custom. They had wrapped the body in linen clothes with 75 pounds of spices (myrrh and aloes, a gummy substance applied to the wrappings). Jesus' body was in a mummified state. Therefore, any possibility of Jesus not being dead, hiding out in the tomb and then escaping is ruled out.

3. The Surprise of the Women

These women had walked two miles from Bethany. When they left their homes, it was still dark. By the time they arrived at the tomb, the sun had risen. As they walked, they discussed who would roll the stone away so they could pay their last respects to Jesus. This was the greatest tragedy of their lives. They had not come expecting the resurrection but were shocked that they found the stone rolled away and the tomb empty. Their surprise offered further proof because no one was expecting the resurrection.

4. The Stone

All four of the Gospel writers mention the removal of the stone. Mark describes it like this: *". . . they saw that the stone, which was very large, had been rolled away"* (Mark 16:4).

Picture a one-and-a-half to two-ton stone. That's "very large"! The people who prepared the grave perched the stone on an incline. The stone had squared edges, so when they removed the wedge it came crashing down the incline into a groove and covered the doorway. To move it took ten to twenty men. Jesus' body was secure in there.

5. The Empty Tomb

The tomb was empty, the body gone, the graveclothes lying there. The face covering was folded up in the corner (John 20:7). After the angel spoke to the women, he sent them back to Jerusalem to tell the disciples what had happened.

Let's say all of this is a big lie. Then all that had to happen to silence the lie of the empty tomb was to produce the body. For a moment let's assume that all 500 plus people who saw Him were wrong. Let's say His body was still dead. Since the whole city knew what had happened, isn't it reasonable that one eyewitness, one Jewish religious leader, one Roman soldier, one somebody would come forward and say, "I saw the dead body of Jesus"? No one did.

Professor Paul Maier summarizes the situation: "Where did Christianity first begin? To this the answer must be: 'Only one spot on earth—the city of Jerusalem.' But this is the very last place it could have started if Jesus' tomb had remained occupied, since anyone producing a dead Jesus would have driven a wooden stake through the heart of . . . Christianity, inflamed by His supposed resurrection."[10] If we can't embrace the resurrection intellectually, then we need to continue to examine the evidence, because the evidence is there to support the reality of the resurrection. It has never been refuted!

Our Emotions

The women who came to the tomb made four emotional responses to the resurrection. When they saw that the stone had been rolled away, the tomb empty and the body missing, they remembered what Jesus had told them: *"after three days [I will] rise again"* (Mark 8:31, 32).

• Alarm

They saw the stone rolled away. Hmmm. Slowly they walked toward the grave, peeked inside and saw a gleaming angel. They were too scared to even scream. The word Mark used is "alarmed" (16:6), which means they were so overcome with fear that they could not move—scared stiff.

• Trembling

When they realized the situation—they were standing in a tomb . . . with an angel . . . a body missing . . . and the thought that Jesus might be raised from the dead—they started to tremble, quaking in their sandals.

• Astonishment

Along with their trembling they were "astonished." Beside themselves, they didn't know what to think. They were confused and bewildered.

• Fear

Their fright caused them to be speechless. They experienced a combination of terror and excitement that Jesus might actually be alive.

Like the women, to discover the reality of the resurrection is to become emotionally involved with Jesus Christ! When that reality confronts us and we see it for ourselves, our emotions will overwhelm us and we will never be the same. Our emotions will move us toward Jesus. If we have a cool or apathetic attitude toward Jesus, then we must question whether or not we have met the living, resurrected Christ.

Our Will

Those women lost no time getting out of that tomb. By this time, all of Jerusalem was up. But these ladies did not talk to anybody! They *"fled from the tomb"* (Mark 16:8). What they saw caused them to act. They ran straight to the other disciples, reporting what they had seen and heard.

In the same way, we too must act on the resurrection. An encounter with the resurrected Christ will determine every action we take for the rest of our lives and it compels us to talk about Jesus to others.

Heavy Thoughts:

Looking Inside

The resurrection impacts every facet of our personalities—intellect, emotions and will.
- *With intellectual proof we don't deny reality to believe in Jesus, but we embrace the truth.*
- *When we embrace the resurrection, we get emotionally involved with Jesus.*
- *Experiencing the power of the resurrection will cause us to act and talk about Jesus.*

Our thoughts, feelings and decisions will be determined by the resurrected Christ who now lives in us!

Dear Jesus:

Jesus with skin on:

Appearing Today

"In short, the Gospels do not present the resurrection of Jesus in the manner of apologetics, with arguments arranged to prove each main point, but rather as a shocking intrusion that no one was expecting, least of all Jesus' timorous disciples."[11]
—*Philip Yancey*

Checking It Out

Two French gentlemen were talking, Monsieur Lepeaux and Bishop Talleyrand, who became a statesman and leader of the French revolution. Lepeaux had started a new religion that he felt was far superior to Christianity, and he was very disappointed that he had gained so few converts. He asked Talleyrand what he should do. Talleyrand told him, "I should recommend that you be crucified and rise again on the third day." The resurrection of Jesus turns dead religion into a revolutionary relationship!

"It was early on Sunday morning when Jesus rose from the dead, and the first person who saw him was Mary Magdalene, the woman from whom he had cast out seven demons. . . . Afterward he appeared to two who were walking from Jerusalem into the country, but they didn't recognize him at first. . . . Still later he appeared to the eleven disciples as they were eating together. . . . Then he told them, 'Go into all the world and preach the Good News to everyone, everywhere'" (Mark 16:9, 12, 14, 15, NLT).

Hot Notes:

Getting the Point

Read Mark 16:9-18.

If Jesus did rise from the dead, then the resurrection is the most sensational event in all of history. We have clear answers to the profound questions of God's existence and ours. We know for sure that God exists, what He is like and how we may know Him by personal experience.

If Jesus did not rise from the dead, then Christianity is, as Paul Little said, "an interesting museum piece—nothing more."

From His appearances after the resurrection, we see His invasion into the lives of His disciples and how that revolutionized their lives.

The Reality of His Appearances

Jesus appeared at least ten times after the resurrection. Check these out:

1. Mary Magdalene (Mark 16:9; John 20:11-18)
2. The women returning from the tomb (Matthew 28:8, 9)
3. Simon Peter (Luke 24:34; 1 Corinthians 15:5)
4. Two disciples on the road to Emmaus (Mark 16:12, 13; Luke 24:13-35)
5. The ten disciples gathered in the upper room (Luke 24:36-43; John 20:19-23)
6. The eleven disciples including Thomas (Matthew 28:16-20; Mark 16:14; John 20:24-29)
7. More than 500 disciples (1 Corinthians 15:6)
8. James (1 Corinthians 15:7)
9. Several disciples including Peter, Thomas, Nathanael, James and John (John 21:1-23)
10. Many on the Mount of Olives at the ascension (Luke 24:50-53; Acts 1:6-12)

When we look at these appearances, we have only three choices concerning how we respond to them:

1. An Invention

If these are inventions, someone could have taken a much more clever approach. Sober and nonsensational, they contain the doubts and fears of the disciples. Women, who were looked down on in their society, played a dominant role. The writers of these stories may have been tragically misled and wrong, but we can say for sure they were not trying to pull the wool over our eyes by deliberately misleading us.

2. An Hallucination

Psychologists agree about what conditions must exist to have a hallucination. Let's see if these events fit that profile:

- Only certain types of persons hallucinate–usually paranoids or schizophrenics. (However, Jesus appeared to 500 at one time who all claimed to have seen the same thing.)
- Hallucinations are highly individualistic because their source is the subconscious mind of that individual. Little likelihood exists that two people would have the same hallucination at the same time. (Yet Jesus appeared to a variety of groups of people.)
- Hallucinations center around an expected event. Usually the person has thought about and desired that event for a long period of time. (Jesus' disciples not only were not expecting Jesus' appearances, they didn't even believe it when they saw Him—Mark 16:11-14.)
- Hallucinations occur in favorable circumstances. They happen only when the time, the place and the mood is right. (The resurrection appearances had great variety—various times, places and moods such as weeping, fear, doubt and disbelief.)
- Hallucinations recur regularly over a long period of time. (Jesus' appearances occurred over forty days, ended abruptly and never occurred again.)
- Hallucinations have no objective reality. (In Jesus' appearances, we must account for things like the empty tomb, the large stone, the graveclothes—all very real objects). Obviously, we cannot put Jesus' resurrection appearances in the hallucination category.

3. The Truth

Canon Westcott, a brilliant scholar at Cambridge University, drew this conclusion about the reality of the resurrection: "Indeed, taking all the evidence together, it is not too much to say that there is no historic incident better or more variously supported than the resurrection of Christ."[12]

The appearances of Jesus after the resurrection offer overwhelming evidence that Jesus *did* rise from the dead. In fact, once we examine the evidence, it takes more faith *not* to believe in the resurrection than to believe in it.

The Faith to Believe

Jesus appeared several times, but the other disciples would not believe it. Jesus was alive but what happened was beyond the disciples' frame of reference. Jesus didn't like their response, so, *"he rebuked them for their lack of faith and their stubborn refusal to believe those who had seen him after he had risen"* (Mark 16:14). They simply could not see it. And if they couldn't see it, they wouldn't believe it.

All of us are like that. Take this little test to see how limited you are in your ability to see. How many times does the letter "F" appear in the following sentence? "Finished files are the result of years of scientific study combined with the experience of many years."

How many times did you have to count until you got six? They were all there all the time; you just couldn't see them. The facts of the resurrection are there. Now what will it take for us to put our faith in them?

Jesus says, "Believe!" To understand what that means, we must see the difference between intellectual understanding and life commitment. Intellectual understanding is taking a few facts about Jesus and stuffing them into the glove compartment of my car labeled "religion," then barreling down the highway of life with "me" in the driver's seat and no apparent change of direction for the car.

Life commitment is taking the facts about Jesus and staking everything on the belief that Jesus is who He says He is. It means getting out of the driver's seat completely, so He can take control, and allowing the car to take a different direction. The facts are there, but have you staked it all on the resurrection to the degree that you are willing to let Jesus take total control of your life?

Availability to Be Used

Once the reality of the resurrection sets in, the entire direction of our lives changes. Once the disciples "believed," then Jesus challenged them in a major way. He said, *"Go into all the world and preach the good news to all creation"* (Mark 16:15).

Once we believe, Jesus' challenge to us is the same—to take the good news to the whole world. Following Jesus is not a spectator sport! You are either a missionary or a mission field!

But we don't feel prepared for the mission. "I couldn't do that," you say. But Jesus gives us resurrection power to do the job—power over the supernatural forces of evil (Mark 16:17); power to communicate (Mark 16:17); the power of God's protection (Mark 16:18); the power to heal (Mark 16:18); and the power of Jesus' continuing presence.

"Then the disciples went out and preached everywhere, and the Lord worked with them and confirmed his word by the signs that accompanied it" (Mark 16:20).

Heavy Thoughts:

Looking Inside

Jesus appeared after His resurrection—that's reality. *Are you willing to risk your life on the resurrection of Jesus Christ?*

We believe in Him—that's faith. *Will you receive the power of the resurrection that Jesus has made available to you?*

We spread the good news—that's availability. *Will you ask God to use you to take the good news of the resurrection to your world?*

Just like He did through the disciples, Jesus wants to demonstrate His resurrection power through you! He can do things through you that you never dreamed possible!

Dear Jesus:

Jesus with skin on:

Surprise!

"Unexpected surprises give us hope in the midst of a scary, chaotic world. The resurrection of Jesus Christ is just the surprise we needed to bring us from sin, fear and insecurity into safety, forgiveness and wholeness before God."[13]
—Joey O'Conner

Checking It Out

My daughter Katie had needed a car for over a year. But we didn't have the money to get one. I knew what she wanted: a dark green Toyota Camry, four doors, gold trim, tan interior—"but it doesn't have to be new, Dad." When we talked about it, she would say, "Dad, I know we can't afford it, so whatever you get will be okay with me." Her sweet attitude motivated me.

That's why I was pumped when she came out of her dorm room and her mom and I were standing there beside her dark green Toyota Camry with four doors, gold trim and tan interior holding the keys with a balloon and "Happy Birthday" sign attached. She couldn't say anything. She walked around it. She hugged us and cried, but words would not come.

I loved that surprise! So did Katie! Jesus pulled off a surprise bigger than that on two of His disciples after the resurrection.

"That same day two of Jesus' followers were walking to the village of Emmaus, seven miles out of Jerusalem. As they walked along they were talking about everything that had happened. Suddenly, Jesus himself came along and joined them and began walking beside them. But they didn't know who he was because God kept them from recognizing him."

"As they sat down to eat, he took a small loaf of bread, asked God's blessing on it, broke it, then gave it to them. Suddenly, their eyes were opened, and they recognized him. And at that moment he disappeared! They said to each other, 'Didn't our hearts feel strangely warm as he talked with us on the road and explained the Scriptures to us?'"
(Luke 24:13-16, 30-32, NLT).

Hot Notes:

Getting the Point

Read the whole episode in Luke 24:13-35.

A surprise is something sudden and unexpected that brings astonishment. Jesus' encounter with the two men on the road to Emmaus certainly qualifies as a surprise.

The Same But Different

On their trip to Emmaus, the two disciples walked and talked about everything that had happened. Then "suddenly" Jesus joined them walking along beside them. Surprise! Not really, because they did not recognize Him. Catch this: the resurrected Christ walked beside people and it didn't even phase them because they didn't know who He was. Luke 24:16 says, *"but they were kept from recognizing him."*

Have you ever been in a situation where you were supposed to recognize someone, but didn't? At a reunion I saw a guy I knew well in high school. When he spoke to me, I had no clue. That's because he was bald, wore horn-rimmed glasses and had gained 80 pounds! No wonder I didn't recognize him.

Jesus had a new resurrection body. What was it like? We will discuss that in depth in the next session, but for now: His body had flesh and bones, and His new, glorified body could act independently of the laws of space and time. With Jesus' glorified body, the disiciples did not recognize Him.

The Fascinating Conversation

Jesus walked and talked with them, but they still had no clue (Luke 24:17). They launched into what was bugging them as Jesus listened. They were extremely discouraged because Jesus' life had been cut short. They described Jesus as a prophet, someone who did wonderful miracles, a mighty teacher, highly regarded by both God and all the people and the Messiah who had come to rescue Israel (Luke 24:19-21). They were upset because this amazing man had been shut down. They lost hope because the expected Messiah was dead.

Take Jesus out of the equation today and hopelessness reigns. People drink, take drugs and kill themselves without the hope of Jesus.

Not only were the two men discouraged, they were also filled with doubt. They said, *". . . some of our women amazed us. They went to the tomb early this morning but didn't find his body. They came and told us that they had seen a vision of angels, who said he was alive. Then some of our companions went to the tomb and found it just as the women had said, but him they did not see"* (Luke 24:22-24).

The word "amazed" (v. 22) means puzzled or doubtful. The men doubted because they couldn't figure out the facts. Three facts confused them: the absent body; the angel who said Jesus was alive; and the empty tomb.

Those three facts have caused people to doubt for centuries—people like Frank Morison. In the 1920s this young British journalist had convinced himself that the resurrection of Jesus was a fable. He decided to do the world a favor and dispose of this superstition once and for all. He decided he would disprove every fact of the resurrection in a court of law. But when he took the resurrection through the legal process, he found that the case was not as easy as he thought. When he finished, he wrote a book, entitling the first chapter, "The Book That Refused to Be Written." In it he described how, as he examined the evidence, he became convinced, against his will, of the validity of the facts of the resurrection of Jesus. The title of the book is *Who Moved the Stone?*

Often we say, "Don't confuse me with the facts." Really, the facts can confuse us sometimes. That happens when we haven't examined the facts thoroughly, we let our feelings cloud the facts, we let our friends encourage us to ignore the facts or we fear having to make lifestyle changes because of the truth discovered.

That is what happened to these two men. They couldn't see God's perspective on the facts and that caused doubt. Only when we get God's perspective on the facts can we move beyond doubt.

Jesus threw in another factor that was giving them problems—disbelief. He said to them, *"How foolish you are, and how slow of heart to believe all that the prophets have spoken! Did not Christ have to suffer these things and then enter his glory?"* (Luke 24:25, 26).The prophets had already spoken, the Christ had died on the cross and the person of Jesus had been clearly revealed in Scripture. So why couldn't they believe? For the same reason we often can't—our God is too small!

The very things that caused them to be discouraged, doubt and disbelieve were the same facts that offered the strongest proof that Jesus was alive! For us those same facts of the resurrection should lift us out of discouragement, doubt and disbelief!

The Veil Removed

What happened that finally caused them to recognize Jesus?

"As they sat down to eat, he took a small loaf of bread, asked God's blessing on it, broke it, then gave it to them. Suddenly their eyes were opened, and they recognized him. And at that moment he disappeared!" (Luke 24:30, 31, NLT).

They recognized Him, not because they knew the facts but because they were broken. Jesus broke the bread as a symbol of His broken body on the cross. And it serves as a symbol of our need to be broken. The psalmist said it like this, *"The sacrifices of God are a broken spirit; a broken and contrite heart, O God, you will not despise"* (Psalm 51:17).

When we allow ourselves to be broken of our self-sufficiency, pride, arrogance, coolness and disbelief, then Jesus will take the veil away and show us more of Himself.

The Burning Heart

Once they recognized Jesus, it all came together. *"They asked each other, 'Were not our hearts burning within us while he talked with us on the road and opened the Scriptures to us?'"* (Luke 24:32).

From broken lives to burning hearts—that's the way it always works! And a burning heart always serves as:

• A magnet to other believers

These two guys walked seven miles to Jerusalem and immediately *"found the Eleven and those with them, assembled together"* (v. 33). People with burning hearts for Jesus want to be together.

• A microphone to tell its story

As soon as they could, *"the two told what had happened on the way, and how Jesus was recognized by them when he broke the bread"* (v. 35). Seeing is believing, and believing is telling! When we encounter the resurrected Christ, we will believe and tell!

Heavy Thoughts:

Looking Inside

God likes surprises! He surprised these two on the way to Emmaus. And He wants to surprise you. He wants to overcome any discouragement, doubt or disbelief in you with the overwhelming reality of the resurrection. That will happen when, like the bread and the two disciples, you allow Him to break you. Then He will put a burning heart in you for Him, for other believers and for telling others about the resurrected Christ.

Dear Jesus:

Jesus with skin on:

The Scars

"Why did Jesus keep the scars from his crucifixion? Presumably he could have had any resurrected body he wanted. . . . The scars are, to him, an emblem of life on our planet, a permanent reminder of those days of confinement and suffering. I take hope in Jesus' scars. . . . Scars never completely go away, but neither do they hurt any longer."[14]
—Philip Yancey

Checking It Out

My friend Ron and I sat in the restaurant. A man walked across the restaurant toward us. The man looked right at my friend. Ron stood up to shake his hand. "How are you? . . . How's the family? . . . the kids? . . . your job? . . . Good to see you." The man then continued on into the men's room. Only then did Ron realize what had happened. He had never seen the man before. He was a total stranger who had just gotten up to go to the bathroom! Trying to be polite, neither of them admitted that they had never laid eyes on each other before!

The opposite is true when Jesus appeared to His disciples. Immediately they recognized Him; all but Thomas, that is.

"On the evening of that first day of the week, when the disciples were together, with the doors locked for fear of the Jews, Jesus came and stood among them and said, 'Peace be with you!' After he said this, he showed them his hands and side. The disciples were overjoyed when they saw the Lord" (John 20:19, 20).

Hot Notes:

Getting the Point

Read this fascinating account in John 20:19-29. Two scenarios play out in the resurrection drama that give us even greater conviction that the resurrected Jesus is real.

1. Jesus appeared to ten disciples (verses 19-23).

Filled with fear and hopelessness, the disciples quaked in their sandals. They knew that if the Jewish leaders found them, they would be dead ducks. They thought that what the leaders did to Jesus they would do to them. That's why the disciples were meeting behind locked doors. Everyone was gloomy and scared.

Then four factors turned their gloomy, fearful world upside down.

• Jesus' Spiritual Body

Locked doors did not limit Jesus. He came through the doors and stood among them because He had His glorified body. The moment Jesus was raised from the dead His body changed. He could appear and disappear. He vanished out of sight when He ate with the two men in Emmaus (Luke 24:31). He was not always recognized at first sight (John 20:14). He had a spiritual body—one so controlled by the Holy Spirit that the Spirit could do with it whatever He wanted with unlimited possibilities. His body operated beyond the limits of time and space. The apostle Paul described this spiritual body as imperishable, glorious, powerful, incorruptible, immortal and victorious (1 Corinthians 15:42-57).

• Jesus' Human Body

Mysteriously, not only did Jesus have a glorified body, but He still had a human dimension too. He still had flesh and bones. When He showed His disciples His hands and side, they knew it was Him because of the scars. They recognized Him by His physical features. Several times they were invited to touch Him (Matthew 28:9; John 20:27). In Luke 24:39 Jesus said, *"Touch me and see; a ghost does not have flesh and bones, as you see I have."* The Bible teaches the physical reality of Jesus' resurrected body. A spiritual body + a physical body = a glorified body.

When the disciples encountered Jesus in His glorified body, they moved from fear to joy!

• Jesus' Mission

Jesus had completed His task. He had done all the Father had sent Him to do. He passed the baton to the disciples. *"Peace be with you! As the Father has sent me, I am sending you"* (John 20:21). His mission became the disciples' mission. Before they followed Jesus but with no clear understanding of His purpose. At this point they understood that His purpose was, and still is, to proclaim the resurrected Christ!

• Jesus' Power

It's one thing to have a mission; it's another to have the power to carry it out. Jesus did not leave them powerless. He breathed His Spirit into them and told them, *"Receive the Holy Spirit"* (John 20:22). Jesus offered His disciples four power points—ways His power affected them then and now affects us.

- Power comes from the life of Jesus breathed into us.
- Power comes by receiving the Holy Spirit.
- Power comes to those who understand who Jesus is. Earlier Jesus had said, *". . . the Spirit will reveal to you whatever he receives from me"* (John 16:15, NLT).
- Power comes as we use the authority He has given us. Jesus said, *"If you forgive anyone his sins, they are forgiven; if you do not forgive them, they are not forgiven"* (John 20:23). As we use His power, He gives us more power.

An amazing transaction took place. The *fearful* disciples were transformed into *fearless* disciples. They had everything they needed to turn the world upside down. And so do we!

2. Jesus appeared to Thomas (verses 24-29).

Enter: Doubting Thomas! Who was this guy who has gotten such a bad rap? He was one of the 12 disciples, called "the Twin." He was absent when Jesus appeared to the other disciples. Thomas got a bad reputation from this one sentence: *"Unless I see the nail marks in his hands and put my finger where the nails were, and put my hand into his side, I will not believe it"* (John 20:25).

What's so bad about that? The truth is we need more people like Thomas. Most people don't doubt enough! Many students go through the religious motions. They act apathetic and uncommitted. Why? Could it be they never asked enough questions like Thomas asked? Did they accept Jesus because everybody else did? Could it be that they never had to struggle with their decision to follow Christ? Did it come so easily they took it for granted?

Most doubters are not in Thomas's class. They are proud to be skeptics. They have no interest in the evidence. Their minds are closed. But Thomas had honest doubt. The difference between honest and dishonest doubt is that honest doubt is looking for a way to believe. That's Thomas!

Remember this about *Doubting* Thomas: he became *Believing* Thomas! Most people remember that Thomas doubted but most forget that he believed.

A week later the same disciples were in the same house. They had the same doors locked. And the same Jesus came through the wall in His same glorified body. He said exactly the same words, *"Peace be with you!"* (John 20:26). Jesus set Thomas up! He set up the same situation as a week earlier so Thomas could experience Him like the other disciples did. Jesus offered Thomas three challenges to help him overcome his doubt:

• Jesus offered proof.

The very proof Thomas demanded, Jesus gave him. He invited Thomas to *"Put your finger here; see my hands. Reach out your hand and put it into my side"* (John 20:27).

• Jesus demanded commitment.

Once Jesus supplied the evidence, He put the challenge to Thomas, *"Stop doubting and believe"* (v. 27).

• Jesus deserved worship.

And Thomas gave it to Him. Thomas responded to the challenge by proclaiming, *"My Lord and my God!"* (v. 28). That is the exact response Jesus wanted from Thomas. He personalized the resurrection. Since people don't rise from the dead just every day, and since the One who was dead was now obviously alive, Thomas had only two responses he could make—disbelieve the evidence or believe the evidence. He chose to believe. Then he fell on his knees and worshiped Jesus.

Heavy Thoughts:

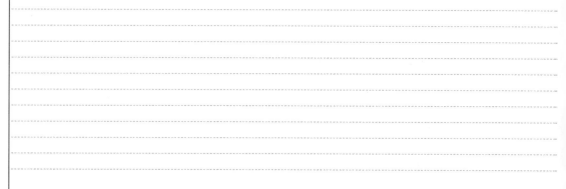

Looking Inside

The disciples struggled to believe because they were hopeless and afraid. Thomas struggled to believe because of his doubt.

What struggles do you have with your faith? From what you have learned here, what do you need to do to overcome those struggles?

"Then Jesus told him, 'Because you have seen me, you have believed; blessed are those who have not seen and yet have believed'" (John 20:29).

Dear Jesus:

Jesus with skin on:

Gone Fishin'

"The power of the resurrection is the power of personal regeneration. Resurrection is not just a passport to heaven, but a power to change us now." [15]
—Lloyd Oglivie

Checking It Out

My seventy-year-old Aunt Ethel came to spend the night with us. She had never visited our house before. We put her in the guest room. She and my son, Jonathan, who was about four at the time, got to be good buddies very quickly. After we had gone to bed, and Aunt Ethel was sound asleep, Jonathan got up in the night and walked into her room. He got right up in her face in the dark and stood there—breathing on her. Who knows how long he did that. But after a while she woke up, and it scared her right out of her pajamas!

Jesus kept showing up in the face of His disciples like that! They didn't know when or where He would appear. And when He did, it frightened them. But they knew it was Him.

"'Now come and have some breakfast!' Jesus said. And no one dared ask him if he was really the Lord because they were sure of it. Then Jesus served them the bread and the fish. This was the third time Jesus had appeared to his disciples since he had been raised from the dead" (John 21:12-14, NLT).

Hot Notes:

Getting the Point

Read John 21:1-25.

Jesus was not a figment of someone's imagination, an hallucination or a ghost. He was a real person "breathing in the face" of His disciples. The Jesus who had beaten death and come back to life stood in their presence and revealed His purpose for their lives!

Catching Fish

Seven of the disciples were "hanging out" because they didn't know what else to do with themselves. Peter, the big fisherman, told them, "I'm going fishing." And the others decided to go with him. They fished all night, but they caught nothing. Then Jesus showed up.

"At dawn the disciples saw Jesus standing on the beach, but they couldn't see who he was. He called out, 'Friends, have you caught any fish?' 'No,' they replied. Then he said, 'Throw out your net on the right-hand side of the boat, and you'll get plenty of fish.' So they did, and they couldn't draw in the net

because there were so many fish in it. Then the disciple whom Jesus loved said to Peter, 'It is the Lord!'" (John 21:4-7, NLT).

Either darkness or the glorified body of Jesus kept the disciples from recognizing Him. Then John realized who it was. *"When Simon Peter heard that it was the Lord, he put on his tunic [for he had stripped for work], jumped into the water and swam ashore"* (John 21:7, NLT).

Like all fishermen, Peter was wearing a loincloth while he fished, but then he put his tunic (long shirt) on because he knew the Jewish law that you must be clothed to greet someone. Peter put on his tunic because, eager beaver that he was, he wanted to be the first to greet Jesus.

When they got to shore, Jesus had prepared a breakfast of fish and bread. Jesus invited them to bring some of their fish to cook. When they counted what they caught, they had 153 fish and the net had not torn.

Why is this story so important? Because it shows us again how authentic the resurrection is. Jesus did not exist because of the vivid imagination of the disciples, or the wild hallucinations of some emotionally unstable people. Rather, Jesus existed after the resurrection as a real person. He had a real body that built a real fire, cooked real fish and then really ate it.

Feeding Sheep

After they had finished eating breakfast, Jesus had a serious talk with Peter. To grasp the impact this conversation had on Peter, we have to understand that Peter was the loudest, wildest, craziest of all the disciples.

• Jesus asked for Peter's past—the good and the bad.

Over all of his loud protests that he would not do this, Peter had denied Jesus. He had told Him that if everyone else abandoned Jesus, he would not. Within a few hours, a teenage girl intimidated him. He went on to deny Jesus three times (Matthew 26:69-75). That was Peter's worst nightmare.

Around the fire Jesus gave Peter a second chance! Here Jesus turned Peter's life around. Through this encounter with the resurrected Christ, Peter moved from denial to destiny, from defeat to victory.

Jesus asked Peter a question: *"Simon son of John, do you truly love me more than these?"* (John 21:15). By that question Jesus could have meant two things: Perhaps Jesus swept His hand around the boat, the nets, the equipment, even the fish—and was asking Peter if he was ready now to give up everything important to him in order pursue Jesus and His goals for Peter's life; or Jesus could have looked around at the rest of the disciples while He was asking the question. Jesus took him back to that night around another fire, when Peter denied Him. Jesus gently reminded Peter that he once thought he could do it in his own strength and do it alone, but he couldn't.

Either way Peter humbly responded to Jesus as a man who knew he was weak, and without promising Jesus anything, he answered: *"Yes, Lord, you know I love you"* (John 21:15). Jesus wants us to give Him the pain of our past too.

• Jesus restored Peter.

Notice how many times Jesus asked Peter the same question (see vv. 15-17). Remember how many times Peter had denied Jesus? Three. By asking Peter the question three times, He probed deep into his heart and gave him an opportunity to receive forgiveness for each of the times he denied Jesus. Jesus gave Peter the opportunity to wipe out the three denials with three expressions of love. In the same way Jesus wants to forgive and restore us.

• Jesus loved Peter unconditionally.

When Jesus asked the question "do you *love* me?," He used the Greek word *agapé* to show His total, unconditional love for Peter. Jesus offered Peter the love that had caused Him to go to the cross. Peter's deep wound of denying Jesus had to be healed. His confidence had been shaken. He insisted that he loved Jesus in spite of his conduct, and Peter expressed his love for Jesus three times by saying, *"Lord, you know all things; you know that I love you"* (v. 17).

Jesus loves us the same way He loved Peter—with total, unconditional love. And He wants us to love Him with deep affection.

• Jesus showed Peter his life purpose.

Each time Peter told Jesus he loved Him, Jesus looked him in the eye and told him, *"Feed my sheep"* (vv. 15-17). Jesus was asking Peter to take care of God's people—to love them, tend to them and to make sure they are fed. Peter's purpose for the rest of his life was to take care of Christ's sheep.

But Jesus went beyond that great purpose. He told Peter that he would die for Christ. And what Jesus said came true. Peter did die—on a cross. But before they nailed him to the cross, Peter asked to be nailed upside down, because he was not worthy to die as Jesus had died.

When we tell Jesus that we love Him, we need to know that He will accomplish His unique purpose for us—and it will cost us our lives.[16]

Heavy Thoughts:

Looking Inside

The resurrected Christ comes to us like He did to Peter and the disciples. He wants to take all of our past—the good and the bad. He desires to restore us by giving us His total unconditional love. Then He plans to launch us into His purpose for our lives. The main question we have to answer is the one Jesus asked Peter: *"Do you love me?"*

Dear Jesus:

Jesus with skin on:

"You ascended from before our eyes, and we turned back grieving, only to find you in our hearts."
—St. Augustine

Checking It Out

During a riot in a large city with the noise of gunshots and fires in the streets, a young girl woke up from her sleep. What she heard, and saw scared her. She called to her mother, who was out of the house. By the time her mom arrived, she was in tears. Her mother tried to calm her: "It's okay. Jesus is here with you." The girl said to her mother, "Yes, but I wanted somebody with skin on."

Jesus empowered His disciples, and us, to become Jesus with skin on.

"But you will receive power when the Holy Spirit comes on you; and you will be my witnesses in Jerusalem, and in all Judea and Samaria, and to the ends of the earth" (Acts 1:8).

Hot Notes:

Getting the Point

What happened after Jesus completed His appearances to His disciples was absolutely incredible—He ascended into Heaven. Through that, He provided the way for us to be Jesus with skin on!

Jesus' Ascension

Jesus' ascension into Heaven offers us even further proof of the resurrection and the power that came from it. Luke told about the ascension at the end of his first book (Luke) and continues it at the beginning of his second book (Acts).

He wrote, *"In my former book, Theophilus, I wrote about all that Jesus began to do and to teach until the day he was taken up to heaven, after giving instructions through the Holy Spirit to the apostles he had chosen. After his suffering, he showed himself to these men and gave many convincing proofs that he was alive. He appeared to them over a period of forty days and spoke about the kingdom of God. On one occasion, while he was eating with them, he gave them this command: 'Do not leave Jerusalem, but wait for the gift my Father promised, which you have heard me speak about. For John baptized with water, but in a few days you will be baptized with the Holy Spirit'"* (Acts 1:1-5).

The ascension had to happen! If it hadn't, would Jesus have wandered around for thousands of years in His glorified body? Would the resurrection appearances have just diminished until Jesus disappeared? Somewhere, sometime, a day had to come when the Jesus of Earth became the Jesus of Heaven. The ascension was that day. For the disciples it ended their relationship with the Jesus in the flesh and began their relationship with the Jesus of the Spirit. Were the disciples sad? Hardly.

"Then they worshiped him and returned to Jerusalem with great joy" (Luke 24:52).

What makes Jesus' ascension so important? Before the ascension Jesus told His disciples "the plan." It had such importance that all four of the Gospels and Acts repeated it.

Matthew: *"Therefore go and make disciples of all nations, baptizing them in the name of the Father and of the Son and of the Holy Spirit, and teaching them to obey everything I have commanded you. And surely I am with you always, to the very end of the age"* (Matthew 28:19, 20).

Mark: *"Go into all the world and preach the good news to all creation. Whoever believes and is baptized will be saved, but whoever does not believe will be condemned"* (Mark 16:15, 16).

Luke: *"This is what is written: The Christ will suffer and rise from the dead on the third day, and repentance and forgiveness of sins will be preached in his name to all nations, beginning at Jerusalem. You are witnesses of these things. I am going to send you what my Father has promised; but stay in the city until you have been clothed with power from on high"* (Luke 24:46-49).

John: *"'Peace be with you! As the Father has sent me, I am sending you.' And with that he breathed on them and said, 'Receive the Holy Spirit'"* (John 20:21, 22).

Acts: *"But you will receive power when the Holy Spirit comes on you; and you will be my witnesses in Jerusalem, and in all Judea and Samaria, and to the ends of the earth"* (Acts 1:8).

After Jesus went up to Heaven, He gave His disciples (and us) three significant tools we need in order to live the Christian life:

1. The Power of the Holy Spirit

Jesus gave the Holy Spirit so He could live in us, empowering us to live the Christian life. The Holy Spirit is the third person of the Trinity—the Father, Son and Holy Spirit. He is the personality of Jesus living in each of us. When He lives in us, He gives us three "power tools":

• The fruit of the Spirit (Galatians 5:22, 23)

The Holy Spirit produces fruit—love, joy, peace, patience, kindness, goodness, faithfulness, gentleness, self-control. These are the characteristics of Jesus living in us by the Spirit.

• The gifts of the Spirit (Romans 12:4-8; 1 Corinthians 12:4-11; Ephesians 4:11-13; 1 Peter 4:10, 11)

God gives each of us spiritual gifts in order to do His work through us. Using our spiritual gifts, we can bring the power of Christ into any situation.

• The boldness of the Spirit (Acts 1:8)

This boldness makes us witnesses. A witness is someone who lives a life that reflects Jesus, loves friends by embracing them for Jesus and tells His story so that others can see Jesus in a real way.

The power of the Holy Spirit in the disciples (the gifts, character and boldness) turned the world upside down in a matter of a few years. And the same Spirit in you can turn your world upside down. The Holy Spirit makes us Jesus with skin on!

2. The Purpose of Witnessing to the World

Looking at Jesus' words in Matthew 28:18-20, we see what Jesus had in mind when He told His disciples to evangelize the world. Jesus said He had "all authority." He gives His authority to us to carry out His purpose. That authority is like a policeman directing traffic. If I stood in traffic blowing a whistle, cars would run over me. But when the policeman blows it, everyone obeys because he has the authority of the entire government behind him. Because Jesus lives in us, we wear His authority like the policeman's uniform. His authority belongs to us in every situation.

Jesus said, "as you are going," make disciples. That means "since you are going to school anyway," make disciples. We go because Jesus told us to go. We have no other option if we want to obey Him. He is not sending us there alone. He is already there and invites us to join Him. Right now He is working in our friends' lives. He put you there for the most important witnessing opportunity of your life. Go!

He called us to make disciples. A disciple is a follower. Our job at school is to help others become radical followers of Jesus. Every page in Acts tells how the disciples "gossiped the gospel." They told everyone, everywhere about the resurrected Christ. Every conversation focused on Jesus. Now God wants to empower you to gossip the gospel at your school!

And we are called to reach "all nations." The church multiplied so much that in Acts 17:6 their enemies claimed they had *"turned the rest of the world upside down"* (NLT). If we communicate our faith and help new Christians become strong disciples, God will multiply our individual influence. With all of us doing that, He will accomplish His final goal: *"a vast crowd, too great to count, from every nation and tribe and people and language, standing in front of the throne and before the Lamb"* (Revelation 7:9, NLT).

(Some additional resources by Barry St. Clair that will help you carry out the Great Commission are *Taking Your Campus for Christ*, *Pole 2 Locker* and *Getting Started*.)

3. The Promise of His Return

Jesus' ascension gave us a promise that Jesus would return and take us to Heaven to be with Him. Until then, what is He doing? John 14:2 says He has gone to *"prepare a place for you."* Hebrews 10:12 says He has *"sat down at the right hand of God."* He looks after our interests in Heaven and on earth. Hebrews 7:25 says He *"always lives to intercede"* for us. He is waiting until the entire world hears the gospel before He returns in a blaze of glory. *"And this gospel of the kingdom will be preached in the whole world as a testimony to all nations, and then the end will come"* (Matthew 24:14).

Heavy Thoughts:

Looking Inside

Jesus ascended into Heaven, then He released His Holy Spirit into the lives of believers. Through the Holy Spirit, believers have the power of God in their lives, the purpose of God to communicate Christ to the world and the promise that someday Jesus will return.

How does that affect your life? What does that motivate you to do? What changes do you need to make? How can you be "Jesus with skin on"?

"And be sure of this: I am with you always, even to the end of the age" (Matthew 28:20, NLT).

Dear Jesus:

Jesus with skin on:

Coming Attraction

"Tomorrow's history has already been written . . . at the name of Jesus every knee must bow."
—*Paul E. Kauffman*[17]

Checking It Out

The most awesome responsibility of the most powerful office on earth settled in on the shoulders of the young president-elect. At his father's house in West Palm Beach, Florida, he worked on final plans for the New Frontier. For recreation he could have invited a fellow statesman, another powerful politician, an entertainer or a relative. But he had something on his mind. Instead he invited a clergyman for a game of golf. As they sat in the front seat of the car after the golf game, John F. Kennedy looked searchingly into the eyes of Billy Graham. "Billy, would you tell me about the second coming of Jesus Christ? I don't know much about it." Forty-six brief months later, in November 1963, Cardinal Cushing answered that question before millions of people mourning the assassinated president.

That day Cardinal Cushing read these words:

"For the Lord himself will come down from heaven, with a loud command, with the voice of the archangel and with the trumpet call of God, and the dead in Christ will rise first. After that, we who are still alive and are left will be caught up together with them in the clouds to meet the Lord in the air. And so we will be with the Lord forever" (1 Thessalonians 4:16, 17).

Hot Notes:

Getting the Point

Read about Christ's second coming in 1 Thessalonians 4:13—5:1-11.

The second coming is mentioned about 1,845 times in the Bible and 318 times in the New Testament. Seven of every ten chapters in the New Testament make reference to the second coming. Yet rarely do we discuss it today. Why? Most people don't like to think about it, glossing over it with a comment like, "I hope He waits till I'm married and have kids." Or they dismiss it as some theological discussion about the future that doesn't relate to where we are now. Or maybe it just seems vague and confusing.

But we need to look at Christ's second coming as an extension of what happened at the resurrection and ascension and as the greatest coming attraction in history!

The Blessed Hope

Emil Brunner said, "As lungs survive by oxygen so Christians survive by hope." The apostle Paul called the second coming *"the blessed hope"* (Titus 2:13). What does that hope look like?

• Hope in Jesus

The basis of our hope is Jesus Christ. Our hope hinges on all of the things we have looked at over the last several weeks—the life, death and resurrection of Jesus. His crucifixion and resurrection provide the vital link to hope. We move past Jesus' death and resurrection to hope for our own death and resurrection when we take seriously what Paul said: *"We believe that Jesus died and rose again and so we believe that God will bring with Jesus those who have fallen asleep in him"* (1 Thessalonians 4:14).

• Hope for the Dead

The Thessalonian church was looking for the second coming of Jesus any day. Some had started dying off. They had expressed concern that those who had died would be left behind. The apostle Paul addressed that issue clearly for them and us when he said, *"God will bring back with Jesus all the Christians who have died"* (1 Thessalonians 4:14, NLT).

• Hope Through Our Grief

Life is full of grief. But because we know Jesus is coming again, the sting is removed so that we do not *"grieve like the rest of men, who have no hope"* (1 Thessalonians 4:13). I have total hope that one day I will see my Dad again! Jesus' resurrection and second coming give me that hope.

The Breakthrough from Heaven

In the dome of the Capitol in Washington, D.C., the designer inscribed these words: "One God, one law, one element, and one far-off divine event to which the whole creation moves." That "divine event" is the second coming of Jesus. Since it is so important, let's answer some basic questions about it.

Q: Who is coming?

A: Jesus. We are not waiting for an event. We are waiting for a person (1 Thessalonians 4:16).

Q: How is He coming?

A: *"With a loud command"* (v. 16). This shout refers to a military command given with urgency and authority. We will know it is His voice because Jesus said, "My sheep recognize my voice" (John 10:27, NLT).

• "With the voice of the archangel" (1 Thessalonians 4:16)

The archangel is Michael (see Jude 9). He is God's chief angel. His job now is to handle demons and the devil, so when Jesus returns, Michael will be a happy camper! His shout will be a shout of victory.

• "With the trumpet call of God" (v. 16)

In the Old Testament they used a trumpet to call people to war and to worship. At the second coming, the war will be over and He will call us to worship.

Q: Who is going with Jesus?

A: First, all the Christians who have died will rise from their graves. Then, all who are "in Christ" will go—that's us if we are still alive when He comes. Some people who have attended church all their lives, but do not really know Jesus will be very surprised when they don't go!

Q: How will we go?

A: We *"will be caught up together with him in the clouds"* (v. 17). The phrase "caught up" means to seize or carry off. It comes from the Latin word *rapio* from which we get the word "rapture."

Q: Who else will be there?

A: We will be *"with them"* (v. 17) and with the Lord. Imagine: Peter, Paul, Moses, Elijah, believing Thomas, everyone you know who is a believer—they will all be there.

Q: How long will this last?

A: We will *"be with the Lord forever"* (v. 17). This is the climax of all life and eternity!

Q: When is He coming?

A: We can count on three things:

• He will come suddenly. *". . . the day of the Lord will come unexpectedly, like a thief in the night"* (1 Thessalonians 5:2, NLT).

• He will come to destroy the earth. *"While people are saying, 'Peace and safety,' destruction will come on them suddenly, as labor pains on a pregnant woman"* (1 Thessalonians 5:3).

• He will allow no one to escape. *". . . and they will not escape"* (1 Thessalonians 5:3).

The Behavior of Believers

What should we do until Jesus comes? Try to figure out when it will happen? No. Paul says we should live as children of the light (1 Thessalonians 5:4, 5). By the time we know He is coming, it will be too late to prepare. Because of how quickly He will come, the apostle Paul tells us what we need to do.

• Keep awake, alert and sober.

"So then, let us not be like others, who are asleep, but let us be alert and self-controlled" (1 Thessalonians 5:6). Paul paints a picture of a soldier on sentry duty. He is armed and dangerous. He listens for every sound. He stands ready and prepared. To be ready for Jesus to come, we must be spiritually alert.

• Think clearly about our salvation.

"But let us who live in the light think clearly, protected by the body armor of faith and love, and wearing as our helmet the confidence of our salvation" (1 Thessalonians 5:8, NLT).

• Encourage one another.

"Therefore encourage one another and build each other up, just as in fact you are doing" (1 Thessalonians 5:11). We are responsible to challenge, exhort and hold accountable our fellow Christians, so they, too, will be ready for Jesus' return.

Heavy Thoughts:

Looking Inside

The only way to behave in a way that will prepare us for the second coming is *"through our Lord Jesus Christ"* (v. 9). He died for us and rose again to give us the strength we need to live for Him. Martin Luther expressed it best: "We are to live and work as though Jesus Christ died yesterday, rose today and is coming again tomorrow."

Our prayer should be the prayer at the very end of the Bible:

"Amen. Come, Lord Jesus!" (Revelation 22:20, NLT).

Dear Jesus:

Jesus with skin on:

Knowing Jesus

If being cocky and self-sufficient when I was in high school wasn't bad enough, I also used people to accomplish my goals. That arrogant, know-it-all person was one side of me—the real side. The other side of me was the nice guy, who was friendly to everybody and who went to church every Sunday. I was a leader in the church youth group. I knew a lot about the Bible. And I could act religious when the situation called for it.

I was like the little boy who came running into his house one day yelling, "Mommy, Mommy, look!" He was carrying a dead mouse with him, dangling it by the tail. "I killed him, Mommy," he blurted out. "I ran over him with my bike, then I hit him with my baseball bat, my soccer shoe, and my football . . . " About that time, the boy realized that the preacher had come to visit. Suddenly an angelic look came across the boy's face as he finished his sentence, ". . . and the little mouse went home to be with the Lord."

That's the way I lived my life in high school. I could be religious when I was in church on Sunday. But Monday through Saturday, Christianity had little effect on the way I lived. A lot of people live that way. It's easy for them to act like Christians in church. But the rest of the time, their lives demonstrate that they don't really know Jesus Christ in a personal way.

The apostle Paul *knew* Jesus! In his letter to the Philippians, Paul described the change that had taken place in his life. He said, *"But all these things that I once thought very worthwhile—now I've thrown them all away so that I can put my trust and hope in Christ alone. Yes, everything is worthless when compared with the priceless gain of knowing Christ Jesus my Lord"* (Philippians 3:7, 8, TLB).

For Paul, knowing the facts about Jesus Christ wasn't good enough. He wanted a dynamic, personal relationship with Jesus. It's having that kind of relationship that makes Christianity come alive. When you date someone, you can learn all kinds of facts about that person. But if it's someone you care for, having the facts is nothing compared to going out and spending time with that person. You enjoy being with someone you care for. When you receive Jesus Christ into your life, you begin a relationship with Him. Though it's important to know the facts about Jesus, what's most important is knowing and loving Him more and more as your relationship grows.

To have that kind of relationship with Jesus, Paul set some goals. They're found in Philippians 3:10. Paul wanted to know Christ, the power of His resurrection, the fellowship of sharing in His sufferings and to become like Him.

Getting Personal

"I want to know Christ . . ."
Soon after I got to college, I discovered that I was no longer the terrific success I had been in high school. Since first grade, I had always played basketball. It was a major part of my life. But when I got to Davidson College on a scholarship, I discovered that my scrawny six-foot body didn't play so well against guys who were 6'10", 6'11", 6'12", 6'13"!

I tried hard. I continued to shoot, even though my giant teammates kept smashing the ball back into my face. I kept playing defense, even though my body got plastered to the court on a regular basis. Finally I began to suspect that the goal I had set of making all-conference wasn't very realistic. I've already mentioned what my social life was like during my freshman year—a total disaster—as illustrated by the blind date my second week at school.

I had also set some academic goals. I had decided I was going to be at least a B student. Then my first test came—in history, the subject in which I had planned to major. I studied like crazy. But when the test results came back, I found out I had made a 74, a D. I had never made a D in my life. Being the "we try harder" person that I was, I decided I would just have to study more. I studied twice as hard preparing for the next test. So what grade did I get? Not a 74 but a 47! My academic goals were sliding down the tube fast. It was as if all the props I had depended on were being knocked out from under me.

I remember homecoming weekend. I was lonely, homesick and depressed. The girl I had asked to homecoming dumped me at the last minute. And to make it even worse, just before school began that year my grandmother had died. I was closer to her than anyone else during adolescence. Saturday morning I stared out of my dorm window and asked myself for the first time: "Who am I? What am I doing here? Where am I going?"

I had never seriously considered these questions before. One thing I finally realized was that I was not sufficient in myself. I began to search for answers beyond myself. In the following months, I looked for answers in intellectualism, in philosophy, in relationships, in athletics. The more I searched, the emptier I felt. I finished my freshman year feeling that the entire year had been a waste.

That summer I attended a camp in the mountains of North Carolina. My first day there I met a beautiful girl and decided I wanted to ask her out. I asked her to go to church with me that night, and she agreed. After church, we took a walk down a lonely, dark road. We talked for a while, then I started to ease my arm around her to kiss her. "No," she said firmly.

No girl had ever done that to me before. Flustered, I did something dumb. I asked her, "Why not?"

"Because of Jesus Christ," she shot back.

I remember standing there in the dark, scratching my head and thinking, *"What does Jesus Christ have to do with kissing?"* Only later did I understand that a relationship with Jesus affects every area of life—especially that area! This girl intrigued me. I saw something different in her, a quality of life that I hadn't seen in other girls I had dated. Somehow I understood that she knew Jesus Christ in a way I had never known Him.

At the same camp, I met a basketball player from the University of Tennessee. We spent a lot of time in the gym together. Soon I realized that he had that same relationship with Christ that this girl had. The two of them talked to me and influenced me to think seriously about my relationship with Jesus Christ.

In that search I made some great discoveries! God loves me. God loves me more than I love myself (and that was a lot!). God would love me if I were the only person in the world. God proved His love for me. Romans 5:8 says, *"But God demonstrates his own love for us in this: While we were still sinners, Christ died for us."*

My search led me to the Bible, and I began to grasp the truth of verses like this one: *"God showed how much he loved us by sending his only Son into the world so that we might have eternal life through him. This is real love. It is not that we loved God, but that he loved us and sent his Son as a sacrifice to take away our sins"* (1 John 4:9, 10, NLT).

The influence of my two new friends, my own searching and the unseen working of the Holy Spirit led me to a decision. One night I knelt beside a chair and prayed, "Jesus, I've called myself a Christian for a long time, but I need You to become real to me. I want You to come into my life the way You've come into the lives of my two friends. I want to know You. Make me what You want me to be."

And Jesus did come into my life! There was no thunder or lightning, no trumpets, no angels, only a calm peace that came over me. It wasn't an emotional experience, but it was real. That was when I began to get to know Jesus.

Power Jam

"I want to know Christ and the power of his resurrection . . ."

One day, about a year and a half after that prayer in my dorm room, the thought came to me, *"Barry, maybe you shouldn't be playing basketball."* My next thought went something like this: *"St. Clair, that's about the dumbest idea you've ever had."*

Everything in my life revolved around the game. I wanted nothing more than to play college basketball and, hopefully, to make all-conference. Quitting was out of the question. So I pushed the thought out of my mind. But the thought kept coming back, *"Maybe you shouldn't be playing basketball."* One day I was reading the Bible and came across Matthew 6:33: *"But seek first his kingdom and his righteousness, and all these things will be given to you as well."*

"Seek first what God wants," the verse seemed to say to me. And I had to admit, *"Barry, you've been a Christian for a year and a half. But you've never offered to give up basketball to God—never."*

God seemed to be asking, "Are you serious about Me?" I knew He wanted me to give up the most important thing in my life. Or at least to be *willing* to give it up. But I wasn't sure I was willing. Just the thought of giving up basketball made me sick.

For several weeks I struggled with the issue. I remember sitting in my parents' car one Saturday morning. We talked, cried and prayed over this. I sensed that to obey God I needed to give up basketball—scholarship and all. It was serious business, but I believed God wanted me to do it. And I did.

That experience was a significant turning point for me. Right then I began to discover the resurrection power of Jesus Christ in my life. I began to grow spiritually—and to know Jesus—much more than ever before. The key to the new power I was experiencing was one simple word: obedience. God wanted me to obey Him, and when I did, I began to experience the kind of power in my life that He wanted me to have.

God wants every believer to experience this power—the same power that raised Jesus from the dead! Jesus wants to change us. And He changes us through His resurrection power working in us. Paul wrote, *"I pray that you will begin to understand how incredibly great his power is to help those who believe him. It is that same mighty power that raised Christ from the dead and seated him in the place of honor at God's right hand in heaven"* (Ephesians 1:19, 20, TLB).

That power is in every Christian, because Jesus lives inside every believer. His resurrection power works in us as we obey Him. Jesus said, *"Whoever has my commands and obeys them, he is the one who loves me. He who loves me will be loved by my Father, and I too will love him and show myself to him"* (John 14:21).

The fact that I quit basketball does not mean that's what God wants everyone to do! What He really wants is our hearts. For me, obedience to Jesus meant giving up the hours I spent eating and sleeping basketball. For someone else, it may mean making a relationship right with parents. It may involve a boyfriend or girlfriend, popularity or some habit. But until we are willing to obey Jesus completely, we won't really know Him or the power of His resurrection.

The basketball story has a significant footnote: two years after I gave up basketball, the Lord gave it back to me. I had the opportunity to travel with Athletes in Action, an all-Christian team that competes against major colleges and universities. We used basketball to share the message of Jesus with people who came to the games. In one summer I traveled to five countries—Japan, Korea, Taiwan, Hong Kong and the Philippines—playing 50 games in seven weeks. At every game, my teammates and I had the opportunity to tell fans and players about Jesus Christ.

Once I gave basketball over to God, He gave it back to me—not for my glory but for His! That's resurrection power at work!

Hard Times

"I want to know . . . the fellowship of sharing in his sufferings . . ."

Some people have the idea that becoming a Christian makes all of life's problems disappear. Baloney! God never promised that the Christian life would be "easy street." In fact He promised just the opposite. *"For it has been granted to you on behalf of Christ not only to believe on him, but also to suffer for him"* (Philippians 1:29).

Many people discover that they have more problems after they receive Christ than before. That's because becoming a Christian brings us into conflict with the world. Following Jesus generally means taking life more seriously. We get involved in sticky situations like speaking out against injustice and standing up for truth when the truth is not popular. But on the positive side, these pressures push us closer to Jesus and cause us to grow stronger in Him. We may have more problems, but we also have the problem solver!

Several years ago my wife, Carol, and I were having a wonderful time at a beautiful conference center near Asheville, North Carolina. But I had a nagging, frustrated feeling that I couldn't shake. God seemed light years away from me. For several months before the conference, this miserable feeling had been gnawing at me, and it all came to a head during the conference.

The Lord brought to mind a certain sin in my past that I had never confessed to Him or tried to make right. I had thought about the incident before, but I had never admitted to myself that it was a problem. I hadn't even been able to tell Carol about it. This time I realized that the problem had to be taken care of.

First I confessed the sin to the Lord. I knew He forgave me, but further action was needed. I told Carol what had been bothering me. "When I was in college, I cheated on some German tests. Deep down inside, for a long time, I've known that was wrong, but I couldn't admit it. Now I know that if I'm going to be the person God wants me to be, I need to get this problem straightened out."

When Carol and I returned home, I called the German professor. Talking to him was the last thing in the world I wanted to do. I was nervous; I had sweaty palms and sweaty pits! What scared me most was that I could lose my college degree—but I knew it was the right thing to do. "Doctor," I said, "I cheated on some of your tests. That was wrong. Will you forgive me?"

He said, "Sure, Barry, I forgive you."

It was one of the hardest things I've ever done in my life. But I can't express the feeling I had when I finished apologizing and hung up the phone. I felt as if a weight had been lifted. I almost floated out of the room. I was free!

Through this experience I began to understand a little bit about what the *"fellowship of his suffering"* is all about. Many people around the world suffer greatly, even at the cost of their lives, for the cause of Christ. Doing the right thing—what Christ wants—sometimes means Christians have to pay a price.

When we are willing to face up to the hard things and meet them head-on, God can deal with the problems in such a way that He sets us totally free from them. John 8:36 says, *"So if the Son sets you free, you will be free indeed."* So many believers never experience freedom from the things that keep them bound. They stay in their miserable conditions because they aren't willing to pay the price required to straighten out their problems. They're not willing to go through the cross—the suffering—in order to get to the resurrection—the power that sets people free.

But as Christians we have the privilege of identifying ourselves with the cross of Christ, as Paul did. He wrote, *"I have been crucified with Christ and I no longer live, but Christ lives in me. The life I live in the body, I live by faith in the Son of God, who loved me and gave himself for me"* (Galatians 2:20).

Identifying with the cross means more than wearing one on a chain around our necks. It means facing up daily to the problems that confront us. It means dealing with our problems and issues the way Jesus wants us to deal with them—no matter how much it may hurt. You never experience the resurrection till you go through the cross. You never experience the power till you go through the suffering.

Chipping Away

"Becoming like him . . ."
In stating his fourth goal, Paul said, I want to become *"like him [Christ] in his death"* (Philippians 3:10). Some people believe that Paul was referring to the spiritual process of dying to self, so that Christ's resurrection power could work in him. Others believe that Paul wanted so much to be like Jesus that he would consider it an honor to die physically in the same way Jesus died—on the cross. Either way, it's obvious that one of Paul's main goals was to *be like Jesus.*

Someone asked a famous sculptor to explain how he had made a statue of a horse. The sculptor answered, "You just take a piece of granite and then chip away everything that isn't a horse." As we get to know Jesus, and experience the power of His resurrection and the fellowship of His sufferings, God begins shaping us to be like Jesus. He begins to chip away at certain areas of our lives that prevent us from being like Jesus. And sometimes it's painful. But the areas that God takes away are those that keep us from reaching the goal He has in mind for us.

God has a plan, a blueprint, for our lives. He wants to make us like His Son. *"For from the very beginning God decided that those who came to him—and all along he knew who would—should become like his Son"* (Romans 8:29, TLB).

That doesn't mean that God clones us. To become like Jesus doesn't mean we lose our individuality. Just the opposite is true. He changes us so that we all resemble Jesus, but each with our own unique twist. We become His unique work of art (Ephesians 2:10). We discover our unique selves in Christ. Cloned, no. Changed, yes. God is at work in us day by day to make us like His Son—knowing Him, experiencing His power, suffering for His sake.

Up Close and Personal

1. In what way can someone know about Jesus without really knowing Him personally? What are some things you know about Jesus? Would you say you know Him personally? How do you know?

2. Can you think of a time you experienced Jesus' resurrection power as a result of obeying Him?

3. Is there some unconfessed sin in your life that's keeping you from experiencing Jesus' resurrection power? Why not confess it now?

4. Consider the example of a potter and clay. If God were sculpting you to make you like His Son, what attitudes and actions would He have to "chip away" from you? In what ways has He already sculpted you to resemble Jesus?

The Lordship of Jesus

Jumping Hurdles

"The Son of God became the Son of Man that the sons of men might become the sons of God."
—Author unknown

Checking It Out

At a track meet I watched my son's friend try the hurdles. He had never jumped hurdles before. The gun went off. He flew out of the blocks leading the race—until he got to the first hurdle. He jumped, but way too early. He came down with one leg on one side of the hurdle and the other leg on the other side. Ouch! He then fell headfirst onto the asphalt track, leaving behind the skin on his hands, legs and nose! Double ouch! He quit track the next day.

We face hurdles that keep us from knowing Jesus more intimately. The writer of Hebrews tells us how to handle them.

"Therefore, since we are surrounded by such a great cloud of witnesses, let us throw off everything that hinders and the sin that so easily entangles, and let us run with perseverance the race marked out for us. Let us fix our eyes on Jesus, the author and perfecter of our faith, who for the joy set before him endured the cross, scorning its shame, and sat down at the right hand of the throne of God. Consider him who endured such opposition from sinful men, so that you will not grow weary and lose heart" (Hebrews 12:1-3).

Hot Notes:

Getting the Point

According to these verses, in life's race we have a finish line—a goal: JESUS! We are told to fix our eyes on Him. But lots of things get thrown in our path every day that keep us from pursuing that goal. How do we jump those hurdles and *"run with perseverance the race marked out for us"* (Hebrews 12:1)?

Hear the Cheerleaders

Like a huge, energetic crowd yelling at the stadium, we have people who are cheering for us. Who are they? We can't see them. They are the *"great cloud of witnesses"* (v. 1) who are in Heaven now. How encouraging to know that people like the apostle Paul, Martin Luther, Mother Teresa, Rich Mullins and even godly grandparents stand on the edge of Heaven cheering us on every day. GO! GO! GO!

Jump the Hurdles

Hurdles are designed to trip us up! But we need to jump over the ones that do. What hurdles do we face that wipe us out? These seven have caused me trouble. Which ones give you trouble too?

1. Do you have impure thoughts toward the opposite sex?

Studies show that guys have thoughts about sex every 29 seconds! It's impossible to escape the lust hurdle, but you can jump it. God's Word says, *"Run from anything that stimulates youthful lust. Follow anything that makes you want to do right. Pursue faith and love and peace, and enjoy the companionship of those who call on the Lord with pure hearts"* (2 Timothy 2:22, NLT).

How does that verse instruct us to get over this hurdle?

- *Run from temptation.* Don't hang around when you are tempted.
- *Aim at Jesus Christ.* He is *"faith and love and peace."* Develop such a passion for Him that your sexual passions are under His control!
- *Find pure friends.* If your boyfriend or girlfriend causes you to stumble, break off the relationship. If other friends cause you to give in to temptation, then find new ones.

2. Do you gripe, complain or have a bad attitude?

How many times in the last 24 hours have you said something like, "I hate your guts!", "You're a jerk!" or "Shut up!"? How do we jump the bad attitudes hurdle?

"In everything you do, stay away from complaining and arguing, so that no one can speak a word of blame against you. You are to live clean, innocent lives as children of God in a dark world full of crooked and perverse people. Let your lives shine brightly before them" (Philippians 2:14, 15, NLT).

Our attitude, more than anything, causes us to "shine"—to reflect Jesus Christ to other people. How do we do that?

- *Don't complain.* Overcome an ungrateful attitude by not griping about what you don't have.
- *Don't argue.* Arguing puts everybody in a bad mood. Choose not to do it.
- *Live clean.* Choose words and actions that reflect Christ.

Nowhere do bad attitudes reflect themselves more than in your relationship with your parents. Read on!

3. Do you respect, honor and obey your parents?

We have two options with our parents: We can *rebel*, saying, "Nobody tells me what to do!" or we can *relax*, saying, "I'll allow my parents to be my parents." We can *relax* when we take seriously these words: *"Children, obey your parents in the Lord, for this is right. 'Honor your father and mother'—which is the first commandment with a promise—'that it may go well with you and that you may enjoy long life on earth'"* (Ephesians 6:1-3).

In our homes with tension and problems, we have to answer this question if we want it to work: "Will I do what my parents want, instead of what I want?"

4. Do you lie, steal or cheat?

Did you know that 75% of all high school students cheat? That makes sense. Lying is what Satan does (see Genesis 3:1-4). That's because he is "the deceiver." But we are made in the image of Christ, not Satan. That's why we don't lie.

"Do not lie to each other, since you have taken off your old self with its practices, and have put on the new self, which is being renewed in knowledge in the image of its Creator" (Colossians 3:9, 10). If you are tempted to lie or cheat, take the following steps:

- *Be honest.* Tell yourself the truth about it.
- *Confess it to God.* He will help you.
- *Ask forgiveness.* Go to those you have lied to and cheated and say, "I lied to you. Will you forgive me?"

5. Is bitterness keeping you from forgiving another person?

Has your best friend ever rejected you? Mine did. It hurts! What do you do?

Jesus pulls no punches when He says, *"If you forgive those who sin against you, your heavenly Father will forgive you. But if you refuse to forgive others, your Father will not forgive your sins"* (Matthew 6:14, 15, NLT).

If anger and bitterness weigh you down, then:

- *Tell God about your hurts.* Since He was rejected, He understands your rejection.
- *Ask Him to heal you.* We know that *"by his wounds we are healed"* (Isaiah 53:5). Let the Wounded Healer heal you.

6. Have you treated another person wrongly?

Maybe you are the one who has rejected and hurt someone else. If so, Jesus tells you what to do: *"Therefore, if you are offering your gift at the altar and there remember that your brother has something against you, leave your gift there in front of the altar. First go and be reconciled to your brother; then come and offer your gift"* (Matthew 5:23, 24). In other words:

- *Remember.* Think about your past and present relationships. Write down the names of anyone you have hurt.
- *Reconcile.* Go to that person and confess what you did. Say, "I hurt you by _____. Will you forgive me?"
- *Return.* Come back with a clean conscience and worship God freely.

7. Do you have idols that keep Jesus from being number one in your life?

An idol is anything that is more important than Jesus to us—a boyfriend or girlfriend, sports, popularity, grades, a habit. Do you have any idols in your life now? Because Jesus knows how easy it is to have idols, He made it clear how to fix the problem. He said, *"But seek first his kingdom and his righteousness, and all these things will be given to you as well"* (Matthew 6:33). Take these steps:

- *Give your idol to Jesus.* Anything more important than Jesus needs to be turned over to Him now.
- *Put Jesus first in your life.* Tell Jesus that you want Him to be number one in your heart.
- *Enjoy the great things He will give you.* He promises that when you put Him first He will give you what you wanted and more.

Which hurdles do you need to jump? Maybe one or maybe all of them. For sure you can't do it in your own strength. But if you decide to jump, Jesus will get you over!

Focus on the Finish Line

Since only Jesus can get us over the hurdles and since He is the finish line, we need to keep our focus on Him constantly. Why?

- ### He is the Author and Perfecter of our faith.
  He began the race . . . finished the race . . . experienced everything we will ever experience in the race. Whatever hurdles we have to jump, He jumped them before us.
- ### He endured the cross.
  Nobody has faced a bigger hurdle than that!

- **He sat down at God's right hand.**

  After bursting out of the grave, eventually Jesus ascended into Heaven and sat down at God's right hand. That means He possesses the power and releases it to us to get us over any hurdles we face. That's why the Hebrews writer says, *"Consider him . . ."* (12:3). Think about Him. Meditate on Him. Talk about Him. Keep Him on the top of your brain and the tip of your tongue!

Heavy Thoughts:

Looking Inside

Listen! The crowd roars, "Go! Go! Go!" The hurdles are set! The gun goes off! The goal is in front of us! Jump the hurdles and don't let anything keep you from reaching the goal!

"Run in such a way as to get the prize" (1 Corinthians 9:24).

Dear Jesus:

Jesus with skin on:

"I can promise that Christ will be all you need. Strength for your weaknesses. Light for your darkness. Peace for your confusion. Food for your hunger. Water for your thirst. Life for your death. And hope for your despair."
—Source unknown

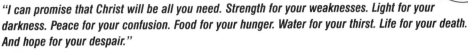hecking It Out

Running very late for the plane, Bill and I made a mad dash down the escalator at the Atlanta airport. We ran for the train that took us to Concourse A. If we didn't catch that train, we would miss our plane. As we approached, the door began to close. I was ahead of Bill, so I lunged for it. The door closed on me. "No problem," I thought. It would work like an elevator door and pop open. NNNNNOOOOO! Wrong answer.

Half of my body was wedged inside the train, and half of it hung on the outside. The inside half consisted of one arm with a backpack, one leg and my head. The outside half included my other arm holding a suitcase, and my other leg. The train door creased my body and was beginning to cause me pain. It was showing no mercy. Then the nasal, robotic, R2D2 voice intoned, "The door will not close. The door will not close. Someone is caught in the door." I wanted to yell, "That's me! You caught me. Now get me out of this mess!" In desperation I looked for some help in a train full of people. They stared at me, their eyes communicating, "You stupid idiot!" No one took a step to help. Clearly I was stuck, and if the train took off I would be dragged to my death. My friend Bill stepped up, pried the door open, and we both hopped on the train.

The apostle Paul faced the same dilemma in his relationship with Jesus. He was "caught in the door" between depending on his own strength or the power of God. God put a significant problem in his life that "opened the door" to God's grace.

"To keep me from becoming conceited because of these surpassingly great revelations, there was given me a thorn in my flesh, a messenger of Satan, to torment me. Three times I pleaded with the Lord to take it away from me. But he said to me, 'My grace is sufficient for you, for my power is made perfect in weakness.' Therefore I will boast all the more gladly about my weaknesses, so that Christ's power may rest on me. That is why, for Christ's sake, I delight in weaknesses, in insults, in hardships, in persecutions, in difficulties. For when I am weak, then I am strong" (2 Corinthians 12:7-10).

Hot Notes:

Getting the Point

Read 2 Corinthians 12:7-10; John 1:14, 16; and Galatians 2:20.

To throw the door wide open, we need to recognize that the more we rely on our own abilities the less God can work. The opposite holds true too. As I realize my weakness, I release Jesus' strength in me.

Realizing My Weakness

Do you ever act conceited? All of us have the ability to get conceited, just like Paul. But God has His ways of getting our attention and keeping us humble. God gave a "thorn in the flesh" to Paul. Some people think Paul had poor eyesight, or had a stomach ailment. Maybe his thorn was zits or being the parent of teenagers! Nobody knows for sure. But he had done some heavy duty praying about it.

What about you? Do you have anything in your life that is a "thorn in the flesh" to you?

• Maybe it's something physical.

You are too tall, so they call you "tree"; you are too short, so they call you "stump"; you are too fat, so when you sit around the house you literally sit *around* the house; you are too skinny so when you turn sideways and stick out your tongue you look like a zipper; you have feet big enough that you go skiing without skis; you have zits—the kind that make you look like you have two heads; you have such buck teeth that if you kissed someone it would pull their tonsils out.

All kidding aside, you could have some serious physical problem. During the time my son Scott attended junior high and high school, he broke his wrist and collarbone, had surgery on his knee twice, and spent 18 days in the hospital from a staph infection that caused double pneumonia.

• Maybe you're struggling with your social life.

You have suffered the rejection of a friend; people talk behind your back; a boyfriend or girlfriend has dumped you; someone is out to get you; it seems like a certain teacher hates your guts.

• Perhaps your biggest weakness lies in the moral/spiritual arena.

Alcohol tempts you; drugs have an appeal to you; lust burns inside of you; pornography overwhelms you; violent behavior comes raging out of you; God seems like a distant idea to you.

• Perhaps you feel family tensions.

You and your parents constantly yell at each other; your mom and dad are always fighting or they are not yelling because they are divorced; someone is abusing you verbally or physically; or you are dealing with the death of a family member.

These "thorns" will either drive you toward God or away from Him. If you try to handle the problem on your own, the situation will get worse because God's presence will be removed. What is God doing to show you how weak you are? Identify your three major weaknesses:

1. _____

2. _____

3. _____

Now let's see how Jesus relates to those.

Releasing Jesus' Strength

Once we admit how weak we are, then we can experience the Lord's power. When Paul had prayed three times for the Lord to remove the thorn, and He didn't, that's when Jesus spoke to him. He said, *"My grace is sufficient for you, for my power is made perfect in weakness"* (2 Corinthians 12:9).

What is the "grace" Paul is talking about? You can take this definition to the bank: *"Grace is Jesus' supernatural strength in us through the cross and resurrection."* Grace is a face—the face of Jesus. Jesus embodied grace. John writes, *"The Word became flesh and made his dwelling among us. We have* seen his glory, the glory of the One and Only, who came from the Father, full of grace and truth" (John 1:14). Jesus was so full of grace—God's supernatural power, that He totally reflected the glory of God.

In the Old Testament the children of Israel had a place outside their camp called the Tent of Meeting. When they pitched that tent, the glory of God filled it. "Then the cloud covered the Tent of Meeting, and the glory of the LORD filled the tabernacle. Moses could not enter the Tent of Meeting because the cloud had settled upon it, and the glory of the LORD filled the tabernacle" (Exodus 40:34, 35). What happened there? The visible presence and power of God showed up in that tent.

That same glory exhibited itself in Jesus. His life was filled with the very presence and power of God. And guess what? That same "divine energy"—the grace of God—lives inside us as believers. According to John 1:16, Jesus doesn't give you just a little of it either: "From the fullness of his grace we have all received one blessing after another."

God's grace is like stacking books in your locker, one book on top of another, then another and another. He gives as much of it as we need. That's why, when we are weak, He gives more. In fact, the worse your "thorn," the more grace you will receive. The result: the weaker we are, the stronger He is in us.

From this we can discover the "Jesus Principle"—Because of the cross and resurrection:

- We die before we live.
- We become poor before we get rich.
- We become weak before we get strong.
- We humble ourselves before we are exalted.

That's exactly what Paul had in mind when he wrote these life-changing words: "Therefore I will boast all the more gladly about my weaknesses, so that Christ's power may rest on me" (2 Corinthians 12:9). Pray this prayer every day to release Jesus' power in your life:

"Jesus: I can't; You never said I could. But You can; You always said You would."

Heavy Thoughts:

Looking Inside

When we realize how weak we are, we open the door to God's grace. That unlocks for us the unlimited potential of becoming all God made us to be. When we grasp that truth, we will stand in awe at **"his incomparably great power for us who believe. That power is like the working of his mighty strength, which he exerted in Christ when he raised him from the dead and seated him at his right hand in the heavenly realms" (Ephesians 1:19, 20).**

Dear Jesus:

Jesus with skin on:

The Big Swap

"Miss Christ and you miss all."[1]
—*Thomas Brooks*

Checking It Out

The Plymouth Valiant looked like an upside-down bathtub. I had paid $400 for it. At one time it was red, but when I got it, it had turned a grayish orange. It had electric windows that rolled down, but not up. So when it rained I had to put cardboard in the windows. Because it had rained inside, I had mildew growing in the back seat of the car. Once I drove it through the snow with loose chains. They beat against the fenders so that the car looked like it had a bad case of acne.

What if a guy had come to me and said, "I want to make an even trade. I'll swap your car for my brand-new Porsche?" My response: "No way! I'm growing mildew in the back seat and I'm going to box it up and sell it." That would have been crazy. Anybody in his right mind would have agreed to that deal.

Our lives are like that old, beat-up Valiant. Jesus is like the brand-new Porsche. What He wants us to do is make the big swap: Swap out your life for His life for the rest of your life.

"For we died and were buried with Christ by baptism. And just as Christ was raised from the dead by the glorious power of the Father, now we also may live new lives" (Romans 6:4, NLT).

Hot Notes:

Getting the Point

Read Romans 6:1-14.

Discovering who we are can cause pain. If we define ourselves by our relationships, then disappointment will follow us all our lives. Why? Because people always disappoint. A breakup with a boyfriend or girl-friend, a parent's divorce, rejection by a friend, abuse from a relative—all of these bring disappointment.

If we determine who we are by our abilities, then frustration will follow us all of our lives. Failing a test, breaking a leg during the season, getting fired from a job, realizing "I just can't do it"—all of these frustrate us by telling us we don't measure up. We need relationships and we must use our abilities, but they don't define who we are. What does?

Self-worth! That's what gives us value and identity. How does it work?
- Self-worth is not about who we are, but about who Jesus is in us.
- Self-worth is Jesus giving us a new identity, a new sense of value.
- Self-worth is not what we do, but what Jesus does through us.
- Self-worth is swapping out our lives for His life.

That's when we find out who God created us to be! How do we get into it? The same way we get into that new Porsche. We open the door and sit in the driver's seat. When we get behind the wheel of a car, what do we do? We put in the key to turn it on, we shift the gears and "put the pedal to the metal." That's exactly what we do to get into who we are in Christ!

Put in the Key of Knowing

We *know* who we are because we were baptized into Christ when we asked Him to come into our lives. The apostle Paul used baptism to illustrate this. He said in Romans 6:3, 4: *"Or don't you know that all of us who were baptized into Christ Jesus were baptized into his death? We were therefore buried with him through baptism into death in order that, just as Christ was raised from the dead through the glory of the Father, we too may live a new life."*

Hang on, we're going into some deep water here! Baptism is a symbol. When a person goes under the water for baptism, it symbolizes the fact that Christ died. But it also symbolizes that the person died. *"For we know that our old self was crucified with him so that the body of sin might be done away with, that we should no longer be slaves to sin—because anyone who has died has been freed from sin"* (Romans 6:6, 7).

Check this out: We were crucified with Christ (when He died, I died); sin was done away with (sin has been smashed in my life—it's dead and gone); we are no longer slaves to sin (it has no more power over us); we are free from sin (we don't have to be involved in it anymore). Wow! That's good stuff! But that's only half the story. We need to get that person out from under the water before he drowns.

Coming out of the water symbolizes the fact that Christ rose. But it also symbolizes that I rose. Paul says, *"Now if we died with Christ, we believe that we will also live with him. For we know that since Christ was raised from the dead, he cannot die again; death no longer has mastery over him"* (Romans 6:8, 9).

Look at what happened: When Jesus rose from the dead, God put life back into Him; when we receive Christ, God puts the life of Jesus in us. The bottom line is this: Christ died and I died; Christ rose and I rose. I am in Christ and Christ is in me. Now I have a new identity!

Shift into the Gear of Trusting

In math the answers never vary. They are always the same. $2 + 2 = 4$ always! We can count on that fact every time. We can trust the fact that it is true.

The apostle Paul used math to help us understand more about who we are in Christ. He told us we have some things we can "count on" (a math term) or trust every time. The Bible has given us promises that we can trust. No matter what kind of lies we have believed about ourselves, we must trust what God says about us. We can count on these promises, that we are:

- children of God (John 1:12)
- loved (1 John 4:19)
- forgiven (Ephesians 1:7)
- changed (2 Corinthians 5:17)
- holy (1 Peter 1:15, 16)
- free (John 8:32)
- accepted (Ephesians 1:4-6)
- capable (Philippians 4:13)

And these are only a few of over 300 promises God made to you in His Book! Shift into gear! Count on it! Trust in it!

Press the Pedal of Obeying

It comes down to two choices: We can either press the pedal of disobedience or the pedal of obedience. Romans 6:12, 13 challenges us, *"Therefore do not let sin reign in your mortal body so that you obey its evil desires. Do not offer the parts of your body to sin, as instruments of wickedness, but rather offer yourselves to God, as those who have been brought from death to life."*

Every day we have two choices: We can offer ourselves to sin or offer ourselves to God. Whatever we offer ourselves to, that's what drives us. To put it another way, the decisions we make every day determine who we become. We make our decisions, then our decisions make us!

Put the pedal to the floor! Decide to obey God! And when you do, you'll be looking pretty good in the driver's seat of that new Porsche!

Heavy Thoughts:

(L)ooking Inside

Understanding and acting on who you are in Christ will change your whole life. So make these decisions so that Jesus Christ becomes your new identity:

• *Decide to put in the key of knowing who you are in Christ.*
  Learn this and say it to yourself over and over every day:
  • Christ died and I died.
  • Christ rose and I rose.
  • I am in Christ.
  • Christ is in me.
  • I have a new identity.

• *Decide to shift into the gear of trusting who Jesus says you are.*
  Look up one of God's promises about you every day and memorize it. (See the promises listed on page 157 to get you started.)

• *Decide to press the pedal of obeying Christ.*
  Make the choice to obey Christ every day, no matter what He tells you to do.
  Can you say with the apostle Paul: *"I have been crucified with Christ and I no longer live, but Christ lives in me. The life I live in the body, I live by faith in the Son of God, who loved me and gave himself for me"* (Galatians 2:20)?

Dear Jesus:

Jesus with skin on:

"I have a great need for Christ; I have a great Christ for my need."[2]
—Charles H. Spurgeon

Checking It Out

The summer before my senior year in college I worked at a camp in the woods of Maine. We slept in tents and bathed in the lake. Rustic does not even begin to describe it. The first week all of the counselors were assigned tasks to get the camp ready for the campers. Quickly it became obvious that I had no talent in the handyman routine. The camp had three categories of workers: 1) the skill squad, 2) the goon squad, and 3) the sub-goon squad. No question: I headed up the sub-goon squad. Even today I get cold chills when I drive by Home Depot. But my one claim to fame is the rolltop desk that I stripped and restored. I worked for weeks applying Strip-Eze® to get all the old gunk off and then rubbing oil in to restore its beauty. Every time I go by it I admire my one-and-only handyman work of art.

What I did to that desk is what Jesus does to us. He strips us and restores us.

"Therefore, there is now no condemnation for those who are in Christ Jesus, because through Christ Jesus the law of the Spirit of life set me free from the law of sin and death. For what the law was powerless to do in that it was weakened by the sinful nature, God did by sending his own Son in the likeness of sinful man to be a sin offering. And so he condemned sin in sinful man, in order that the righteous requirements of the law might be fully met in us, who do not live according to the sinful nature but according to the Spirit" (Romans 8:1-4).

Hot Notes:

Getting the Point

Do you have one sin that just keeps getting the best of you? Do you ever find yourself asking, "Why do I keep doing this?" Do you feel like no matter what you do, it still overwhelms you?

All we have learned about Jesus Christ should help us answer those questions. God wants to show us how Jesus can meet our deepest needs. How does He do that? Like turning my gunky rolltop desk into an expensive antique, Jesus wants to remove all the junk in our lives and turn us into an expensive work of art. He uses two steps to do that.

Stripped of sin

What caused that one sin that keeps plaguing you? We have to look back in the Old Testament to see what happened.

1. In God's image

According to Genesis 1:27 God made us in His image:

"So God created man in his own image, in the image of God he created him; male and female he created them."

Later on God said that what He had made was "very good" (v. 31).

2. The fall

Genesis 3 tells about how mankind fell away from God. Adam and Eve believed the serpent's lie. The lie questioned God's character, and they fell for it. All of us have fallen for the same lie since then. We choose to go our own way, rather than God's way. That is what the Bible calls sin.

The results of what happened are horrible. Before, mankind lived in perfect harmony and peace with God. But sin brought these consequences: shame (Genesis 3:7); fear (vv. 8, 9); blame (v. 12); a curse (v. 17); pain (vv. 16, 17); work (v. 19); death (v. 19); and rejection (vv. 22-24).

Sin created an incredible mess. It was so bad that Genesis 6:5 says, *"The Lord saw how great man's wickedness on the earth had become, and that every inclination of the thoughts of his heart was only evil all the time."*

That hurt God so deeply that He was sorry He had made man at all. *"The Lord was grieved that he had made man on the earth, and his heart was filled with pain"* (Genesis 6:6).

Imagine that! God's heart filled with pain! That's how sin makes Him feel. But the problem didn't stop with Adam and Eve. *"Therefore, just as sin entered the world through one man, and death through sin, and in this way death came to all men, because all sinned"* (Romans 5:12).

A cartoon shows several people standing at the door of this house as the man opens the door. One lady says, "We're looking for the source of all evil and we have narrowed it down to this address."

We need to realize that it is not mankind in general who sinned, but you and me in particular. Then we must see what sin has done to us. It has left us with deep longings. We have a pain and longing in our hearts that can't ever seem to be filled. That pain increases by what other people do to us. Sin causes us to make wrong responses to those people and to our circumstances.

Another consequence of sin is that it has left us with wrong strategies. To fill our longings, we use all kinds of devious methods. We want to satisfy our deepest desires. Our response to our relationships and circumstances shows us clearly how deeply sin is rooted inside of us.[3]

How can we solve the sin problem? We have two options:

1. We can try to solve it ourselves.

I can go inside my already warped and perverted self and determine to dig deeper and do better. Or I decide to cover it up the best I can so people won't know how bad I really am.

2. We can allow God to solve it.

I can seek His infinite resources released to me through what Jesus did on the cross and I find cleansing from the *presence* of my sin, forgiveness from the *power* of my sin and freedom from the *penalty* of my sin.

Through Jesus, God did everything to get rid of sin in our lives. Look at how Paul describes it in Romans 8:1-4: He took away all condemnation or blame (the *presence* of sin); He freed us from the power of sin and death (the *power* of sin); and He met the requirements of the law that we could not meet (the *penalty* of sin).

As a result, sin does not have a grip on us anymore. We do not live according to our sinful nature, but according to the Spirit (v. 4).

The one big step that is necessary on our part is to be honest. Each one of us has to be honest about our own sin. Deep down we know how selfish we are. If you don't believe it, just think about the day you got your school annual. Who did you look for first? Your principal? Right. Your teachers? Sure. Even your best friends? No way. You looked for you. All of us are self-centered and sinful.

Jesus gave us clear direction on what to do. He said, *"Repent, for the kingdom of heaven is near"* (Matthew 4:17).

"Repent" means to turn around 180 degrees. When you are driving and realize that you are going in the wrong direction, you can keep going the wrong direction, or you can turn around and go the other direction. Turning around is what it means to repent.

And that is the way followers of Jesus need to think. Our attitude and lifestyle is one of continual repentance. Every day we look for the sinful choices we make, and we turn away from those to make choices that Jesus would make. It means asking the question every day: "What would Jesus do?"

Restored by the Spirit

To give beauty to our lives, we must get rid of sin, but we must also let the Spirit of Jesus restore us. Like my rolltop desk, once it was stripped of the gunk, I applied oil that penetrated the wood and restored the original beauty. So how do we get restored by the Spirit?

Look at it from a cat-hater's point of view. Muffin, our family cat, had an incredible ability to have kittens. At one point she had given birth to 21 of them! And seven of them still lived at our house. Personally, I've never liked cats. Unlike dogs, they are arrogant. They look at you as if to say, "You're a jerk. And I'm in control here." Then they rub against your leg, not like they want anything, just to be obnoxious. Also, they leave hair everywhere. One by one I got rid of those cats until we got down to Muffin. When she had more kittens, I realized she was the source of the problem, so she had to go too. But who wants an old mother cat? Nobody but my Mom, whose name is Kitty and who loves cats. She took Muffin. Whew! What a relief!

Sin is like those cats: It tends to multiply; it's not easy to get rid of; and it keeps appearing, even when you think you have gotten rid of it.

Possibly you are saying, "Hey, I understand what Jesus did on the cross and how He took care of sin. But honestly, I still sin; it multiplies and I have a hard time getting rid of it. What if I still sin?"

Romans 8:9-11 presents three important ways we can solve the sin problem and let the Spirit of Jesus control us:

1. We are not controlled by our sinful nature.

"But you are not controlled by your sinful nature. You are controlled by the Spirit if you have the Spirit of God living in you. (And remember that those who do not have the Spirit of Christ living in them are not Christians at all.)" (Romans 8:9, NLT). Jesus took care of sin on the cross. When we accept Him, our sinful nature is totally powerless (Romans 6:6).

The cat is gone! One night after I got rid of all of those cats, including Muffin, I had a dream that they all came back. I saw the whole gang on my front porch. I woke up in a cold sweat! Then I realized that they really were gone.

Sin is gone! It has no more power over you because of what Jesus did on the cross.

2. The Spirit of Jesus is alive in us.

"Since Christ lives within you, even though your body will die because of sin, you spirit is alive because you have been made right with God" (Romans 8:10, NLT).

Sin still causes us to have hurts, pains, wrong attitudes and wrong responses. We're not perfect. Eventually, sin brings death.

Even though Muffin and her kittens were gone, every time I was wearing dark clothes and sat down in a chair, I got cat hair all over me. Muffin was gone, but the "cat leftovers" were still around. Sin is like that. The power of it has been broken, but it still has an effect on us.

But since Jesus Christ lives in us, our spirits are alive. That means that we are changing from the inside out. So don't let the "cat hair" of sin on the outside bother you. Because the Spirit of Jesus has made our spirits alive, these changes are taking place in us, according to Romans chapter eight:

- We are not condemned (v. 1).
- Our thinking changes (vv. 5, 6).
- We are accepted and loved (vv. 14-16).
- We have a future hope (v. 18).
- We can overcome weaknesses (vv. 26, 27).
- We discover our purpose (vv. 28, 29).
- We enjoy success (v. 31).
- We overcome adversity (vv. 35-37).
- We experience God's love (vv. 38, 39).

3. The Spirit gives life to our bodies.

"The Spirit of God, who raised Jesus from the dead, lives in you. And just as he raised Christ from the dead, he will give life to your mortal body by this same Spirit living within you" (Romans 8:11, NLT).

The Spirit that raised Jesus from the dead pulsates with life inside of us. He is working to change us from the inside out. Eventually what is happening inside changes what we do on the outside.

Here's how this life-changing, behavior-changing Spirit works. Let's say lust is plaguing you. You see a sexy looking girl (or guy) and your hormones kick in. Every time she walks by, your head turns. Why? Your human spirit (controlled by sin) yells to:

All of them turn on your poor body (eyes, in this case) and yell out, "Lust!" So your body does what it's told. You stare and want to do more. You know this is wrong, and you have tried to take care of the problem by yourself, but you have failed. You're hooked on lust and it's only getting worse.

Now let's turn that around. The sexy guy or girl walks by. Your hormones want to kick in. However, this time your head does not turn. Why not? The Spirit of Jesus who lives in you yells to:

All of them turn on your body (eyes) and yell out, "Self-control!" Screeeech! Your body does what it is told by the Spirit. The power of lust is broken. Every time that happens, the lure of lust becomes less and less. That's what Romans 8:9-11 is all about. The cat is gone!

Heavy Thoughts:

Looking Inside

What is the one sin that keeps getting you?
Are you prepared to "repent" (turn 180 degrees) from it?
Are you willing to let the Spirit of Jesus take control of your spirit, intellect, emotions and will?
"So I say, live by the Spirit and you will not gratify the desires of the sinful nature" (Galatians 5:16).

Dear Jesus:

Jesus with skin on:

Get Fired Up!

"The Christ who died for me, rose again to live in me!"[4]
—*Major Ian Thomas*

Checking It Out

Cheerleaders take a lot of abuse. There is at least one cheerleader joke for every pom-pom in America. You've probably heard this one: "Do you know the difference between a cheerleader and a trash can? A trash can gets taken out more!"

And it gets worse. But I love cheerleaders. My daughter cheered all the way through high school. One thing you have to admit about cheerleaders—they have enthusiasm! Energy, excitement, nonstop screaming and yelling. Get fired up!

Do you ever hear yourself say the opposite of that? Have you ever said, "I'm bored," or "I'm apathetic and I don't care"?

Followers of Jesus never need to be bored. We have *enthusiasm*. Enthusiasm literally means "into God" or "God in us." Jesus gives us enthusiasm.

**"And with that he breathed on them and said, 'Receive the Holy Spirit'"
(John 20:22).**

"Don't be drunk with wine, because that will ruin your life. Instead, let the Holy Spirit fill and control you" (Ephesians 5:18, NLT).

Hot Notes:

Getting the Point

What gets us fired up and keeps us fired up—enthused—as Christians? Since enthusiasm means "into God" then *when God gets into us, we get into Him.*

How did God set that up? After Jesus' death and resurrection, God sent the same Spirit that lived in Jesus to live in us. *"Because you are sons, God sent the Spirit of his Son into our hearts"* (Galatians 4:6).

Who is the Holy Spirit?
Three simple facts should help us understand the role of the Holy Spirit in our lives:

1. The Holy Spirit is a person, not an "it."
That means that He cares for us and is sensitive to us. The Holy Spirit knows us better than we know ourselves. Jesus said, *"But the Counselor, the Holy Spirit, whom the Father will send in my name, will teach you all things and will remind you of everything I have said to you"* (John 14:26).

2. The Holy Spirit is the third person of the Trinity.

No one understands the Trinity completely. But one illustration helps us see how the relationship between the Father, the Son and the Holy Spirit works. Barry St. Clair is one person, but I function in three different ways in my family: I am a son to my parents, a husband to my wife and a father to my children. One person, three functions.

3. The Holy Spirit is the personality of Jesus living in us.

When we ask Jesus to come into our lives, He does not stomp into our chests as a physical person. Rather, He enters our lives as the Spirit. The apostle Paul said, *"I have been crucified with Christ and I no longer live, but Christ lives in me"* (Galatians 2:20).

A glove without a hand in it just flops. It has no life, no form. It can't go anywhere or do anything. But when I put my hand in that glove, it has life in it. That hand allows it to get up and go. Why? It has life in it. Without the Holy Spirit, we are like the glove—lifeless. But with the Holy Spirit, we are full of life.

How does the Holy Spirit work in us?

Jesus infuses us with life through the Holy Spirit. That's why we can get fired up and stay that way. How do we get in on that? Ephesians 5:18 tells us: *"Don't be drunk with wine, because that will ruin your life. Instead, let the Holy Spirit fill and control you"* (NLT).

1. Turn away from the negative.

This verse strongly urges us to stay sober. Why? Because Jesus knows alcohol destroys. Think about it: Why do people drink? Not because they like it. In that case they would stop when they got full. They drink because they like the buzz they get. Alcohol changes behavior.

Alcohol, or any kind of sin, has a destructive effect on us. And when we do it, we harm the Holy Spirit in us and squelch our enthusiasm. We can grieve the Holy Spirit (Ephesians 4:30, 31), resist Him (Acts 7:51) and quench Him (1 Thessalonians 5:19).

Sin puts out His fire in our lives! We can see the negative effect of drinking, drugs, partying, having sex and all sorts of other sins on our relationship with Jesus. It has nothing to do with keeping us from having fun. It has everything to do with keeping us close to Jesus and fired up about Him.

2. Turn to the positive.

Ephesians 5:18 fires us up even more: *"Be filled with the Spirit."* The way Paul says this we know he is not messing around. He doesn't say, "If you want to," or "if you feel like it." No option here—it's a command. He realized that the Holy Spirit must be in control. When he says, "Be filled," we see that God does the filling, not us. The Holy Spirit wants to pour Himself into us continually.

To catch the importance of this, check out this dream I had. One year in college I roomed with Bobby Lane, 6'4" high school All-American in basketball. I thought I was good until I played against Bobby. He beat me like a drum. One day after getting trounced, I sat in my chair and had a dream. I dreamed that Bobby and I went to the gym and played one-on-one. I inherited all of the talent of Grant Hill. I dribbled the ball off my knee and kicked it out of bounds to fake him out. I missed a shot just to make him feel comfortable. Then I said, "Get loose, Grant, baby." And he did. I dunked—360 degrees. I hit every shot. When Bobby got the ball and shot, I slammed it so hard he had "Wilson" written across his forehead. I destroyed him. When we are filled with the Holy Spirit, that's the way we operate. It's not a dream. It's reality. We play to our maximum potential. We jam Satan, and we win big!

What happens to us as a result of being filled with the Holy Spirit?

When we allow the Holy Spirit to control our lives, then we experience the dynamic, enthusiastic life of God. The Bible tells us that we will see several things happen in our lives:

1. We produce fruit.

If I plant an apple tree in my yard, what kind of fruit will it produce? Oranges? No way. It produces the fruit of the kind of tree it is—apples. When we allow God to "plant" the Holy Spirit in our lives, then He produces the fruit of the Holy Spirit. (See Galatians 5:22, 23 for the "fruit list.") As we keep on being filled with the Holy Spirit, then the fruit of the Spirit will come out of us.

2. We receive gifts.

These supernatural gifts are given to meet the needs of others around you—both Christians and non-Christians. Paul split the spiritual gifts into three categories in 1 Corinthians 12:4-6:

- *Grace gifts* that motivate us (Romans 12:6-8).
- *Service gifts* that help us minister to others (Ephesians 4:11, 12; 1 Peter 4:10).
- *Working gifts* that manifest themselves through us (1 Corinthians 12:7-11).[5]

3. We possess power.

Like dynamite the Holy Spirit empowers us to boldly speak up for Jesus Christ and to change people's lives (Acts 1:8). When we ask God for the power of the Holy Spirit, then He will release that power through us so everyone we meet will see Jesus in us. It might be expressed in a smile, a simple "hi," picking up a dropped book, speaking out in class, helping a friend, praying for someone or sharing the message of Jesus. In thousands of different ways God can use us to make a difference in other's lives.

Heavy Thoughts:

Looking Inside

To live this out every day, think about breathing. You have been doing it 24/7. Miss five minutes and you're dead! Breathing spiritually is just as important as breathing physically. How does it work? Physically you *exhale* by breathing out the carbon dioxide, then *inhale* by breathing in clean, pure oxygen. Spiritually you *exhale* by breathing out (confessing your sins). Take a look at 1 John 1:9. Then you *inhale* by breathing in. Here's how: *"Be filled with the Spirit"* (Ephesians 5:18).

Do that every day and you will get fired up and stay that way!

Dear Jesus:

Jesus with skin on:

"Keep your life so constant in its contact with God that His surprising power may break out on the right hand and on the left. Always be in a state of expectancy, and see that you leave room for God to come in as He likes."[6]
—*Oswald Chambers*

Checking It Out

Eating is fun, especially a big family meal. Carol goes all out fixing everybody's favorite dishes. Eating is big at our house. But what if, instead of eating, I decided to just hang out around the table? I analyze it: "Tomatoes—strong on potassium. Potatoes—full of carbohydrates. Chicken—good protein. Cereal—great source of fiber." Then I write a report. But I don't eat. I discuss food, but never eat. I would starve to death!

We can hang around the spiritual table and starve to death too! We can go to church, youth group, retreats and camps, but not take in enough spiritual nourishment to keep us strong and healthy. We need regular spiritual meals. When we sit down at the table with Jesus, we need to eat and get full. When we pig out, we become spiritually nourished and healthy.

"For in Christ all the fullness of the Deity lives in bodily form, and you have been given fullness in Christ, who is the head over every power and authority" (Colossians 2:9, 10).

Hot Notes:

Getting the Point

Read Colossians 2:6-10. Then ask yourself this question: "How do I pig out (get full) on Christ?" In other words, how can you experience fullness of life in Him?

Meat and Potatoes

The phrase "in Christ" provides us with the "meat and potatoes" of the meal. The apostle Paul used it to describe his experience with Christ. For example, he used those two words eleven times in Ephesians 1. It means that: we are "in Christ" and He is "in us." Colossians 1:27 says that God has made known the greatest mystery in the universe: *"Christ in you, the hope of glory."* According to Colossians 1:28, our ultimate goal is to be *"perfect [full] in Christ."*

God gives us the gift of fullness of life in Christ. When we have Christ living in us and Christ living around us, we are full, complete, perfect, mature. We don't always act that way, but "in Christ" we are that way! So how do we become who we already are?

Eating Utensils

We use the "knife, fork and spoon" that the apostle Paul provides for us.

• The Knife

The knife cuts through the surface to get to the real nourishment. That's what we need to do to experience fullness in Christ. How do we cut through the surface spiritually? The apostle Paul gives us a cutting tip. *"So, then, just as you received Christ Jesus as Lord, continue to live in him"* (Colossians 2:6).

How did we receive Christ? In simple faith! So how do we live in Him? In simple faith! Let's don't get this complicated. When we wake up every day, we need to pray, "Lord, I believe that You are in me and I am in You. So I trust You to live in me as I walk through the day."

To "live in Him" can also mean to "walk in Him." What happens when we walk with a friend? We get to know each other better. When I met my wife Carol, we lived on campus, so we walked everywhere. I walked behind her to the library before I met her. I followed her there so I could meet her. One night we walked over to the main classroom building where I kissed her for the first time. Every day after that I walked her to and from class. Walking was the way I got to know her. I didn't expect or want anyone else to walk with her. I wanted to do it myself.

That's the way we experience fullness in Christ. We walk with Him every day. We let Him walk with us. We spend time together. How can we do that?

The Walking Challenge: Continue spending 20-30 minutes a day with Jesus in the Bible and prayer after you finish this week. Tell Jesus you want to walk with Him through the day—going where He goes, doing what He does. One tool to help you do this is the *Time Alone with God Notebook*, by Barry St. Clair. You can order this resource from Reach Out Ministries, 3961 Holcomb Bridge Road, Suite 201, Norcross, GA, 30092, www.reach-out.org.

• The Fork

The fork penetrates down into the food and serves it up to our faces. We need to use the fork to experience fullness in Christ. How do we penetrate down deep spiritually? The apostle Paul suggests getting *"rooted and built up in him, strengthened in the faith as you were taught, and overflowing with thanksgiving"* (Colossians 2:7).

Decide to not just stay on the surface, but to dig down deep into Christ. And, as you experience the satisfying spiritual meal that comes from intimacy with Jesus, you will be strengthened and overflow with thankfulness.

The Digging Challenge: Decide to read one chapter in the gospel of Mark every day for the next month. As you read, ask yourself: "Who is Jesus? What does He want me to do?"

After you have finished this Gospel, do the same with Matthew, Luke and then John. What a feast!

• The Spoon

We use a spoon so we don't spill things. Forks and knives don't hold food well. Spoons do. We need to be able to hold on to fullness of life in Christ and not spill it. That's important because many people will challenge our life in Christ and want to rob us of it. The apostle Paul gives us three warnings about situations that will try to shake Christ's fullness out of us, and replace it with something besides Christ. Paul says, *"See to it that no one takes you captive through hollow and deceptive philosophy, which depends on human tradition and the basic principles of this world rather than on Christ"* (Colossians 2:8).

Warning #1: We will find no fullness in intellectual philosophy.

Paul says it is "hollow and deceptive." In Paul's day a group of people called Gnostics rearranged the gospel so only intellectuals could understand it (sounds like school!). Knowledge, as important as it is, is not what fullness in Christ is all about. Fullness is about submitting our minds to Christ and humbly trusting in Him.

Warning #2: We will discover no fullness in traditions.

Paul calls these "human traditions." When we insist on something that has no basis in the Bible, that is a tradition. Many exist that keep us from focusing purely on our relationship with Jesus—like wearing or not wearing certain things, worshiping Mary or needing church buildings to worship God. Some traditions have value because they remind us of Christ, such as taking communion; others detract from Him.

Warning #3: We will not experience fullness from the principles of the world.

That phrase actually means to "put in rows like ABC's." The world wants to line God up in a row and then put Him in a box. The principles of the world miss the point of the wonderful, full relationship we have with Jesus Christ.

The Warning Challenge: Evaluate everything you think, believe and do in light of what you know about Jesus. Look at one area of your life each week over the next several weeks. Here are a few suggestions to help get you started: your attitude toward your parents; your language; your relationship to the opposite sex; your view on abortion; your attitude towards school; your attitudes towards competition, drinking, popularity and friendships.

Heavy Thoughts:

Looking Inside

Our fullness, completeness and maturity come from Christ's fullness in us. When we understand that, we will want to "pig out" on Christ every day. That's when we experience life at its very best.
"**. . . you have been given fullness in Christ**" (Colossians 2:10).

Dear Jesus:

Jesus with skin on:

Growing Up

"To present Christ's lordship as an option leaves it squarely in the category of stereo equipment for a new car."[7]
—*Dallas Willard*

Checking It Out

Have you ever heard yourself say, "I can't wait till . . ."? Till what? Till you turn 15 and get your learner's permit? Then you can't wait until you turn 16 to get your driver's license. When you get that, then you can't wait until you can buy a car. Then it seems like forever until you turn 18 and graduate. Then you can't wait until you're 21 and are a legal adult. Then you can't wait until you get married. And it goes on and on.

We want to get older. But growing up—becoming mature—is so much more than just getting older. The apostle Paul explains it this way:

". . . we will be mature and full grown in the Lord, measuring up to the full stature of Christ. Then we will no longer be like children, forever changing our minds about what we believe. . . . Instead we will hold to the truth in love, becoming more and more in every way like Christ, who is the head of his body, the church" (Ephesians 4:13-15, NLT).

Hot Notes:

Getting the Point

Maturity means receiving enough from Jesus to meet your needs so that you have enough left over to meet the needs of other people. How do you become mature?

Fill Up Your Character Container

Many people think of character as the way we behave—by "being good" or "acting right." But character is not external. It comes from within. It hinges on *"the fullness of Christ"* in us (Ephesians 4:13). We become people of character as we *"grow up into him"* (Ephesians 4:15). Character is who we are.

Picture your favorite plastic cup. (You might be drinking out of it now.) Fill it full of water. Now shake it really hard. What comes out? What's in it! That's what our character is like. As a follower of Christ, what (who) is in there? Jesus, of course. When He lives in us, then we do several things:

• **We take out our old self.**

Picture your favorite plastic cup again. Fill it with rocks. Those rocks are like the sins in our lives. They clutter the cup and make it dirty. We clutter our character when we shut our minds and harden our hearts (Ephesians 4:18). According to Ephesians 4:19, when that happens we don't care anymore about right and wrong, and we give ourselves over to immoral ways and live our lives with all kinds of impurity and greed.

With our minds shut and hearts hardened, we believe lots of lies about ourselves, things like:

- "That's just the way I am." *And God, the Creator of the universe can't change me.*
- "But I wasn't the only one." *Since everybody else does it, it must be okay.*
- "I don't see any harm in it." *Since I'm the final judge, and I don't see anything wrong with it, then surely there must not be anything wrong.*
- "I'll try it just once." *If I do it once, there won't be any consequences.*
- "Who's going to know?" *As long as nobody knows, it's okay.*
- "I don't listen to the words." *What I hear repeatedly won't influence me.*
- "It's no big deal." *The little things I do don't make any difference.*

We clean up our character when we throw off our old evil nature. It is *"rotten through and through, full of lust and deception"* (Ephesians 4:22, NLT). Reach in the cup and start picking out the rocks. Clean up the clutter. Get rid of the junk. How do we do that? Confess our sins. We know that Jesus has already died for them. When we confess them, they are pulled out of our lives and nailed to the cross—gone!

• We put in our new self.

Go back to the plastic cup. Now that the rocks are coming out, fill it with water. Less rocks. More water. Fill it some more—less rocks, more water.

Less sin. More Jesus. That's what character is all about. Our character gets stronger every time we take out a rock of sin and replace it with the water of the Holy Spirit. Ephesians 4:24 challenges us to *"put on the new self, created to be like God in true righteousness and holiness."* We need to keep on asking God to fill us—to release His life in us. When this happens every day, then we receive enough from Jesus to meet our needs. We are growing up in Him!

Spill Over the Top

When the water runs over the top of the cup, it's evident that it is overflowing. When our lives are running over the top with Christ's fullness, we will experience two things that show we are growing up:

• Our behavior changes.

Without Christ, we keep on repeating the same old behavior again and again. But with Christ, our character changes. We will not lie anymore (v. 25); handle anger properly (v. 26); not steal, but instead work hard (v. 28); speak positively to others (v. 29); not grieve the Holy Spirit (v. 30); rid ourselves of bitterness, anger, brawling and slander (v. 31); be kind and compassionate (v. 32); and forgive others (v. 32). Ask the Lord to bring about any of these behavior changes (or others) that you need.

Because Christ lives in us, we now have His character in our lives. The apostle Paul calls it the fruit of the Spirit: love; joy; peace; patience; kindness; goodness; faithfulness; gentleness; and self-control (Galatians 5:22, 23). Ask the Lord to express His character through you every day.

• Our relationships change.

Without Christ maturing and filling us with His character, we will have unhealthy relationships. Noted psychologist Eric Fromm said, "When you need someone, it is impossible to love him." Without Christ, people continually look for someone to fill the void in their lives. They look for love in all the wrong places. But, when we have a close relationship with Jesus, we become whole as individuals. We are healthily independent, because we are in a right relationship with our Creator. Then we can have healthy relationships.

Take this relationship checkup: "I need you, therefore, I love you" = an unhealthy relationship. "I love you, therefore, I need you" = a healthy relationship. We can know we are pursuing healthy relationships when we can affirm these love principles:

• I accept that I am loved.

The apostle Paul says we are *"dearly loved children"* (Ephesians 5:1). Many young people have been deprived of love on a human level, like the girl who told me, "My mom has never told me she loves me." No matter how much or little love has filled your cup on a human level, Jesus wants to fill it to overflowing.

"God has poured out his love into our hearts by the Holy Spirit, whom he has given us" (Romans 5:5). Ask the Lord to show you how much He loves you. Crawl into Jesus' lap and let Him hug you. Remembering your plastic cup, open your heart and let Him pour His love into you.

• I want to love like Jesus loved.

How did Jesus love? *"Christ loved us and gave himself up for us as a fragrant offering and sacrifice to God"* (Ephesians 5:2). Raise one hand in the air. Stretch out the other one. Imagine the love of God coming down through the raised arm, and out to others through the outstretched arm. We are channels of God's love.

Loving and being loved is a wonderful thing. My friend Dave Busby had polio as a boy. He also had cystic fibrosis. Needless to say, athletics was not his thing. But his older brother was athletic. When friends came over to play, Dave would dribble the ball off his gimpy legs. One Saturday morning when he was shooting around with his brother's friends, they made fun of him. When it came time to choose sides, he wasn't afraid he would be chosen last—he didn't think he would be chosen at all!

His brother was one of the captains. He had first choice. He pointed at his little brother and said, "I choose you, Dave." That made such a profound impact on Dave's life that even as an adult, his view of God was colored by his brother's love. Ask the Lord to make you a channel of His love to others.

Heavy Thoughts:

Looking Inside

Healthy relationships and changed behavior come from the character of Christ in us. That character fills up our lives and overflows from Christ's fullness in our hearts. That's God's way of meeting our needs with enough left over to meet other people's needs. And that's what maturity is all about!

Dear Jesus:

Jesus with skin on:

Notes

Introduction

[1]*Mere Christianity* by C. S. Lewis, 1960, The MacMillan Co., New York, NY. Used by permission.

Chapter one

[1]*The Encyclopedia of Religious Quotations*, Frank S. Mead, editor, 1976, Fleming H. Revell Co., Old Tappan, NJ. Used by permission.
[2]*Science Speaks* by Peter W. Stoner and Robert C. Newman, 1976, Moody Press, Chicago.
[3]*Living Quotations for Christians* by Sherwood Eliot Wirt and Kersten Beckstrom, 1974, Harper and Row Publishers, New York.
[4]*Ibid.*
[5]*The Greatest Men in History* by Mark Link, 1971, Argus Communications, Chicago.
[6]Taken from *The Jesus I Never Knew* by Philip Yancey. Copyright © 1995 by Philip Yancey. Used by permission of Zondervan Publishing House.
[7]*Commentary on the Old Testament in Ten Volumes*, volume 7, by C. F. Keil and F. Delitzsch, 1980, William B. Eerdmans Publishing Co., Grand Rapids, MI.
[8]Taken from *The Jesus I Never Knew* by Philip Yancey. Copyright © 1995 by Philip Yancey. Used by permission of Zondervan Publishing House.
[9]*Ibid.*
[10]Taken from *A Man Without Equal* by Bill Bright. Copyright © 1992, revised 1995, by Bill Bright, *NewLife* Publications, Campus Crusade for Christ. All rights reserved. Used by permission.
[11]Taken from *Know Why You Believe* by Paul E. Little. Copyright © 1988 by Marie Little. Used with permission from InterVarsity Press, P.O. Box 1400, Downers Grove, IL 60515.

Chapter two

[1]*100 Portraits of Christ* by Henry Gariepy, 1987, Cook Communications Ministries. Reprinted with permission. May not be further reproduced. All rights reserved.
[2]*A Stone for a Pillow* by Madeleine L'Engle, 1986, Harold Shaw Publishers, Wheaton, IL.
[3]*The Life and Times of Jesus the Messiah* by Alfred Edersheim, 1883, Longmans, Green and Co., Oxford.
[4]This section on revolution adapted from *The Daily Study Bible*, "The Gospel of Luke" by William Barclay. Used with permission of Westminster John Knox Press, Louisville, KY.
[5]Taken from *The Jesus I Never Knew* by Philip Yancey. Copyright © 1995 by Philip Yancey. Used by permission of Zondervan Publishing House.
[6]Excerpted from *God Came Near*, © 1987, by Max Lucado. Used by permission of Multnomah Publishers, Inc.
[7]*Christ in Christmas* by James Montgomery Boice, James Dobson, Chuck Swindoll and R.C. Sproul, 1989, NavPress, Colorado Springs, CO.
[8]Taken from *New Bible Dictionary,* edited by I. Howard Marshall, A. R. Millard, J. I. Packer and Donald J. Wiseman. Copyright © 1996 by Universities and Colleges Christian Fellowship, Leicester, England. Used with permission from InterVarsity Press, P.O. Box 1400, Downers Grove, IL 60515.

Chapter three

[1]*Time* magazine, January 22, 1996.
[2]Taken from *The Jesus I Never Knew* by Philip Yancey. Copyright © 1995 by Philip Yancey. Used by permission of Zondervan Publishing House.
[3]Taken from "The Stories of Jesus" from *The Living Bible*. Copyright © 1971, Tyndale House Publishers, Wheaton, IL.
[4]Taken from *The Holy Spirit* by Billy Graham. Copyright © 1988. Used by permission of Word Publishing, Nashville, Tennessee. All rights reserved.
[5]*Satan Is No Myth* by Oswald Sanders, 1983. Used by permission of Moody Press.
[6]*The Edge of Evil* by Jerry Johnston, 1989. Used by permission of Word Publishing, Nashville, Tennessee. All rights reserved.
[7]*The Word on the Life of Jesus* by Jim Burns, 1995. Regal Books, Ventura, CA 93003. Used by permission.

Chapter four

[1]Taken from *The Jesus I Never Knew* by Philip Yancey. Copyright © 1995 by Philip Yancey. Used by permission of Zondervan Publishing House.
[2]*Ibid.*
[3]*Ibid.*

[4]As quoted in *The Book of Jesus* by Calvin Miller, 1996. Simon and Schuster.
[5]*Gathered Gold—A Treasury of Quotations for Christians*, compiled by John Blanchard, 1984. Used by permission of Evangelical Press, Durham, England. All rights reserved.
[6]*The Night and Nothing* by Gale D. Webbe, copyright © 1964 by Gale D. Webbe. Used by permission of HarperCollins Publishers Inc.
[7]Taken from *In His Image* by Paul Brand and Philip Yancey. Copyright © 1984 by Paul Brand and Philip Yancey. Used by permission of Zondervan Publishing House.
[8]*Gathered Gold—A Treasury of Quotations for Christians*, compiled by John Blanchard, 1984. Used by permission of Evangelical Press, Durham, England. All rights reserved.
[9]Taken from *In His Image* by Paul Brand and Philip Yancey. Copyright © 1984 by Paul Brand and Philip Yancey. Used by permission of Zondervan Publishing House.

Chapter five

[1]"The Empty Tomb Is History," *Christianity Today* by Paul L. Maier, March 28, 1975.
[2]*Christian Life: Its Hopes, Its Fears and Its Close* by Thomas Arnold, 1859, by T. Fellowes, London.
[3]*Therefore Stand: Christian Apologetics* by Wilbur M. Smith, 1943, Baker Book House, Grand Rapids, MI.
[4]*The Encyclopedia of Religious Quotations*, Frank Mead, editor, copyright © 1965. Used by permission of Baker Book House.
[5]*Who Moved the Stone?* by Frank Morison, 1930, Faber and Faber, London.
[6]*Man Alive* by Michael Green, 1968, InterVarsity Press, Downers Grove, IL.
[7]Taken from *Evidence That Demands a Verdict* by Josh McDowell. Copyright © 1971. Used by permission of Josh McDowell Ministries.
[8]Taken from *More Than a Carpenter* by Josh McDowell. Copyright © 1977. Used by permission of Tyndale House Publishers Inc. All rights reserved.
[9]*The First Easter* by Paul Maier, 1973, Harper and Row, New York. Used by permission of Kregel Publications.
[10]*Ibid.*
[11]Taken from *The Jesus I Never Knew* by Philip Yancey. Copyright © 1995 by Philip Yancey. Used by permission of Zondervan Publishing House.
[12]Taken from *Know Why You Believe* by Paul E. Little. Copyright © 1988 by Marie Little. Used with permission from InterVarsity Press, P.O. Box 1400, Downers Grove, IL 60515.
[13]*The Word on the Life of Jesus* by Jim Burns, 1995. Regal Books, Ventura, CA 93003. Used by permission.
[14]Taken from *The Jesus I Never Knew* by Philip Yancey. Copyright © 1995 by Philip Yancey. Used by permission of Zondervan Publishing House.
[15]*The Word on the Life of Jesus* by Jim Burns, 1995. Regal Books, Ventura, CA 93003. Used by permission.
[16]*The Daily Study Bible* by William Barclay, was very helpful in preparing this devotional. Used with permission of Westminster John Knox Press, Louisville, KY.
[17]*Gathered Gold—A Treasury of Quotations for Christians*, compiled by John Blanchard, 1984. Used by permission of Evangelical Press, Durham, England. All rights reserved.

Chapter six

[1]*Gathered Gold—A Treasury of Quotations for Christians*, compiled by John Blanchard, 1984. Used by permission of Evangelical Press, Durham, England. All rights reserved.
[2]*Ibid.*
[3]*Inside Out* by Larry Crabb, 1988. Used by permission of NavPress Publishing. All rights reserved.
[4]Taken from *Saving Life of Christ* by Ian Thomas. Copyright © 1961 by Zondervan Publishing House. Used by permission of Zondervan Publishing House.
[5]For a full treatment of spiritual gifts including a spiritual gifts test, see chapter six of *Life Happens: Get Ready* by Barry St. Clair, 1997.
[6]*My Utmost for His Highest* by Oswald Chambers, 1963, Barbour and Company, Inc., Westwood, NJ.
[7]*Gathered Gold—A Treasury of Quotations for Christians*, compiled by John Blanchard, 1984. Used by permission of Evangelical Press, Durham, England. All rights reserved.

You have just spent time getting to know Jesus. Are you ready to sign the C.H.R.I.S.T. covenant? Read the following, then sign at the bottom:

Because Jesus loves me and I love Him, I will:

Commit

myself to a love relationship with Jesus Christ—through praying, studying His Word, and allowing His Spirit to lead me each day.

—Matthew 22:36-38

Honor

Christ in my moral life—my thoughts, words, actions and relationships.

—1 Timothy 4:12

Respect

my parents and all authorities in my life—with love, honor and obedience.

—Ephesians 6:1-3; Romans 13:1

Involve

myself in encouraging and uniting with other Christians—regardless of race, church or social status.

—Hebrews 10:24, 25

Seek

God through prayer—asking Him daily to bring spiritual awakening to my generation.

—2 Chronicles 7:14

Take

the message of Christ to my school and world—by praying, living and witnessing so that every student has an opportunity to know Christ.

—Acts 1:8

Believing God has a special destiny and mission for me and my generation, I take this challenge, relying on the Holy Spirit. I join young people and youth workers across our country to pray for a spiritual awakening, and to help take the message of Christ to every school and every young person by year end 2000.

_____   _____
Signed   Date

Now that you have encountered Jesus in a powerful way, you are in a great position to introduce Him to others. Why not take a friend through this study? You can get another book at your local Christian bookstore or by visiting www.standardpub.com.

So now what? We need to take Jesus with us no matter where we go. We need to share Him with others. For most of you, that means you need to take Jesus to school with you since that is where you likely spend most of your time. He wants to radically impact the students on your school campus who are desperately in need of Him. As a follower of Jesus, He will make His presence and character known on your campus—through you! Christ on campus. That is the essence of the C.H.R.I.S.T. covenant you just signed.

Did you know that there are hundreds of thousands of young people who are also committed to the C.H.R.I.S.T. covenant and are reaching their campuses for Christ? They are all a part of Challenge 2000, a nationwide alliance of students, youth workers, churches and organizations working together to establish a ministry of prayer, evangelism and discipleship on every middle, junior high and high school in America.

You can be the match that lights a fire on your campus! If Jesus has given you a desire to reach your friends and other students at your school, you can discover your own ministry by starting with any of these action steps that come from the word ALLIANCE.

Begin anywhere you like, but be sure to:

A dopt your school for Christ
L ead your friends to Christ
L aunch a specific ministry to your school
I mpact your school as a campus missionary
A cquire available resources to help start your ministry
N otify everyschool.com and tell your youth leaders what you are doing
C ollaborate and partner with like-minded Christians on your campus
E ngage others in prayer for your school and ministry

Praying for and sharing Christ with your friends is a phenomenal goal. But, you know, you can go beyond that to praying about sharing Christ with every person on your campus. Then imagine what can happen if you have many other Christians joining you!

To impact your campus, here are some resources you need:
• Go to www.challenge2000.org to get started
• Order the ALLIANCE video and "Adopt a School for Christ" resource bag
• Read the book, *Taking Your Campus for Christ*, by Barry St. Clair
• Start praying for your friends and school by using the book, *An Awesome Way to Pray*, by Barry St. Clair
You can find all of these resources including the *1x1x56K Campus Starter Kit* by calling 1-888-ALLIANCE or by visiting www.challenge2000.org.

Keep checking back to www.challenge2000.org to see the latest resources for your use as well as a video that explains what you can do. Click on the "resources" button to check out other tools that may be helpful in your ministry. *Jesus no equal*. I hope He will use you to change the world!